Voices of Forgotten Worlds

Traditional Music of Indigenous People

EXECUTIVE PRODUCER
JEFFREY CHARNO

TEXT COMPILED AND EDITED BY
LARRY BLUMENFELD

FOREWORDS BY
JULIAN BURGER AND
DAVID LEWISTON

MUSIC COMPILED BY
BROOKE WENTZ

PRODUCED IN COOPERATION WITH THE
UNITED NATIONS CENTRE FOR HUMAN RIGHTS

ellipsis arts ...

VOICES OF FORGOTTEN WORLDS

TRADITIONAL MUSIC OF INDIGENOUS PEOPLE

•

PROJECT ASSISTANT • GILBERT ANTONY BONCY
PHOTO EDITOR • LIZBETH ARUM
RESEARCH ASSISTANT • DEREK M. BANDLER

•

A PORTION OF EACH SALE IS DONATED TO
THE UNITED NATIONS CENTRE FOR HUMAN RIGHTS
TO SUPPORT THEIR WORK ON BEHALF OF
THE WORLD'S INDIGENOUS PEOPLE

•

M
1668.9
.I53
1996

•

FOR INFORMATION PLEASE WRITE:
ELLIPSIS ARTS... P.O. BOX 305
ROSLYN • NEW YORK • 11576

•

PRINTED IN THE UNITED STATES ON RECYCLED PAPER

TABLE OF CONTENTS

Forewords

FOREWORDS

JULIAN BURGER

"We know and understand the earth, and we are humble in her presence, because we know, and have known for thousands and thousands of years, that we exist only with her sufferance. We know and understand humans and other living things on this earth, and we know that all living things are related, that the web of life is woven together, and that injury to one part of the web does injury to the whole. This is our world view, the sacred map that guides us through life. It is one of the many contributions that we are willing to share with the world, as a part of the international community and the family of nations."

WILLIAM MEANS
International Indian Treaty Council at the Opening Ceremony of the International Year of the World's Indigenous People, United Nations, New York, December 12, 1992.

Indigenous peoples have been called the guardians of the earth. It is an apt description and goes beyond a mere acknowledgment that indigenous peoples are respectful of nature and the extraordinary wealth of resources which it harbors. Indigenous peoples are also the caretakers of cultures, customs, philosophies and ways of life which stretch far back in time and will carry forward long into the future.

Sometimes also called first peoples, indigenous peoples are the descendants of the original inhabitants of the lands that have been colonized or overrun by others. They include the numerous Native American nations of the United States and Canada, the Aborigines of Australia, the Maori of New Zealand, the Saami of northern Scandinavia, and the Inuit of the Arctic region. Included in the term indigenous peoples are the tribal peoples of Asia and Siberian Russia, the Indians of Latin America and increasingly some of the most vulnerable groups in Africa. In total an estimated 300 million people living in 70 countries are considered by the United Nations to be indigenous. As the traditional owners of some of the last wildernesses ~ the tropical and boreal forests, the savannahs and deserts, the mountain regions, the Arctic and coastal waters ~ indigenous peoples occupy some 10% of the surface of the planet.

In a world growing ever more uniform, the cultural diversity of indigenous peoples represents a lifeline for the future. By adapting to multitudes of different environments and evolving rich social, political and economic ways of life, indigenous peoples have retained cultural alternatives and fought assimilation into the mainstream societies that surround them. Once thought of as somehow lagging behind the high technology and fast-growth of the developed world, indigenous peoples are beginning to receive recognition for their skills in managing vulnerable ecosystems, commitment to sustainable resource development, equitable social and political systems and strong spiritual values. "Maybe," people are starting to ask themselves, "there is something we can learn from them."

This is a welcome change of attitude as our world, with its apparently unquenchable thirst for minerals, timber, living space, water and other natural resources, is pressing in on them now as much as it did in the past. The lands and resources of indigenous peoples are still seen as underutilized and available for our use and exploitation. And as the lands of indigenous peoples are taken away from them, so the profound spiritual link of a people to its territory, ancestors, past and future is broken.

The result has been to deprive indigenous peoples of their means of subsistence and dignity and often turn them into second-class citizens in the states in which they live. Today the condition of indigenous peoples is the worst of any single group in society. In most countries, indigenous peoples suffer the poorest health, the least access to education, the highest rates of unemployment and disproportionately high levels of imprisonment. According to any socioeconomic indicator, indigenous peoples are at the bottom of the social ladder.

Despite these difficulties or perhaps because of the new pressures on their lands and cultures, indigenous peoples have become increasingly active in defending and promoting their rights. They are challenging the destructive models of development which bring for many only greater poverty and a permanently scarred and damaged environment. They are calling for the international protection of their lands, resources and cultures, and of their right of self-determination ~ the right to decide for themselves what their future should be. They are developing their own health, legal aid, child care and welfare organizations; they are opening schools, revitalizing their languages and establishing radio and television stations.

In recognition of the problems faced by indigenous peoples and the vitality of the new international movement for their rights, the United Nations has designated 1993 as the International Year of the World's Indigenous People. A United Nations declaration on the rights of indigenous peoples is being drafted which will recognize their needs. In June 1992, the United Nations Conference on Environment and Development (the Earth Summit) recognized indigenous peoples as key partners in the search for sustainable development; and in June 1993, the World Conference on Human Rights took special note of the situations of indigenous peoples and called for a decade of action in their favor.

Whatever happens in the next ten years, it is certain that a greater understanding and appreciation by the public of the rich and diverse cultures of indigenous peoples is critical. We share the planet together, and we must care for it in partnership. What better alliance than with the guardians of the earth.

Julian Burger, PhD, *is a consultant with the United Nations Centre for Human Rights. He was formerly deputy director of the Independent Commission for International Humanitarian Issues in Geneva, and director of research at the Anti-Slavery Society in London. He has also been involved in the United Nations Working Group on Indigenous Peoples since it began. Burger has written a number of books on indigenous peoples, and has contributed to numerous publications.*

DAVID LEWISTON •••••••••••••••••••••••••••••••••••••

Recently, a friend asked me why I wander the world, recording music. "Because I enjoy it," I replied. But then, as I was playing one of the 40 records I've made in the past quarter century, and loving the music all over again, I realized that this answer was less than accurate: really, I do it because I never know when I'm going to hear music that is completely new to me and magical. Once I had had this experience, I was hooked for life.

I'm often asked how I got started. In the early 1950s while I was a music student in London I heard the Gurdjieff music ~ music of Central Asian inspiration ~ composed by the Russian composer Thomas de Hartmann during his association with the mystic George Ivanovich Gurdjieff between 1917 and 1929. For someone familiar only with the Western classical tradition, this music was completely unexpected, transporting me to deep peaceful inner space. Soon after I completed my conservatory studies, I moved to New York to study composition with de Hartmann. He was unflaggingly gentle and helpful; I was quite insecure and hypercritical of my limited musical abilities; de Hartmann did all he could to defuse this situation and get me focused on composing. After he died in 1956, my interest turned more and more to world music. But listening to recordings, and reading the descriptions of field collectors simply whetted my appetite. By 1966 I could no longer do without the real thing, so I took off for Bali.

The island's music was unforgettable. The recordings and photographs that were available did little to prepare me for what I found: In a palace courtyard I came upon a Gamelan Gong; there were rows of metallophones ~ metal-keyed instruments which remind the visitor of xylophones or marimbas ~ and sets of gongs, some small, others immense. The instruments' wooden frames were ornately carved with mythical figures painted red and gold. Several musicians sat cross-legged on the ground, flanking a solitary flutist. The 25 musicians began to play, and I was transported by a cascade of glittering, shimmering sound.

Another evening, it was the Kecak in the courtyard of the Temple of the Dead, a hundred men dressed in black-and-white checkered loincloths quietly formed three concentric circles around the flickering of light of a great branching wooden torch. Their motionless bodies grew tense and suddenly a wildly syncopated chant broke out, hurling the Kecak on its tempestuous course. On one level the Kecak enacts a story from the Hindu Mahabarata epic, but what riveted my attention was the primal power of the chorus' hypnotic chant, derived from an ancient trance dance.

For me, the music is the best part of a journey. As I become accustomed to an unfamiliar musical idiom, there's the recognition of grandeur beneath the strangeness, and with it, that joy, that opening of the heart, which is the special gift of great music. In the many years of wandering in out-of-the-way places, I've come to feel that there's an exhaustible richness of great music throughout the world.

In so many communities I've heard something memorable ~ in a village, a wedding dance; on a hillside, a love song; in a monastery, incredible chanting.

Music has been my key to making friends in unfamiliar places. I enjoy exchanges within these remote communities, for these people have a special pride in their local music. They take pleasure in bringing forward a popular performer, and finding that he's appreciated by outsiders as well. There have been so many men and women of goodwill who have taken me into their communities. And I especially enjoy being with the musicians ~ in the crucial events during recording, creating an easy atmosphere so that the performers can relax; and later, translating the songs and learning about the musical instruments. There are hardships, of course ~ loneliness, arduous travel, frequently poor living conditions, indifferent food, and debilitating bouts of dysentery ~ but long after they have faded from memory the joy of the music remains.

My 1968 sojourn in Salvador da Bahia in northern Brazil was another pivotal experience, for it introduced me to trance and possession. Brazil's first capital, Salvador has a large population, descended from slaves brought to Brazil by the Portuguese. Candomble, the old African religion, is still a dominant force in Bahia, and I had the good fortune to witness its rites.

Hours of drumming and chanting induce hypnotic trance states in selected women of the sect. While in trance, the women are possessed by *orixas*, the African gods. The musicians and their instruments are essential, for it is the rhythms of the three tall drums and the *agogo* (two hollow iron cones joined together, beaten with an iron pin) which summon the spirits into their chosen vessels. One by one, the women go into trance, each one exhibiting the manifestations of the deity ~ for *Ogun*, god of war, a sword; for *Oxossi*, god of the hunt, a bow and arrow; for *Oxala*, greatest of the gods, a shepherd's staff with small bells. Thus attired, the entranced woman returns to the ceremony, performing the dances characteristic to the deity possessing her. Hours later, as the ceremony draws to a close, the deity withdraws and the human vessel returns to her normal state.

Ever since I witnessed these rites I've come to accept that there is another world, the world of spirits, invisible, intangible, but very real all the same. I still don't understand trance, it's still a very great mystery, but my travels have made me realize that spirit possession is by no means uncommon. It exists, for example, throughout the Himalayas and Karakorams, and the islands of Indonesia.

Another crucial experience was my introduction to the Tibetans and their culture. In 1971 I met a Tibetan lama, Trungpa Rinpoche, in New York. For the first time, I had met someone who radiated compassion impartially, and it changed the course

of my life. How can I put this in words? Trungpa didn't make an effort to be "nice": Rather, it was as though his nature had been transformed so that compassion simply radiated from him, and this compassion was for all, not just the chosen few. Ever since, this quality has been for me the hallmark of an evolving being. He impressed me so deeply that in the following year I set out to travel in the Himalayas. I went first to Dharmsala in India's western Himalayas. Perched on a 6,000-foot-high ridge covered with gnarled rhododendrons, backed by 18,000-foot-high snow-capped granite peaks, there is a community of several thousand refugee Tibetans, who have settled there to live close to the Dalai Lama.

I was really happy in Upper Dharmsala, or Macleod Ganj as this community is known, because I felt a natural unforced warmth from the Tibetans. Every country exerts a unique conditioning on its people: In the case of Tibet, the people are Buddhist, and the most common spiritual practice involves Chenserig, the embodiment of the Buddha's compassion. I'm not suggesting that all Tibetans are enlightened, or even that they are less selfish than others, but when you have a venerated head of state (the Dalai Lama) enjoining his subjects to be kind to one another, it does make a difference.

Better still, I began to meet other lamas who radiated compassion, just like Trungpa, and I became addicted to the bliss of these encounters.

Refugee monks had rebuilt several monasteries in Dharmsala; wherever I walked in the village, I became accustomed to hearing monks chanting, not just in the temples, but also in homes, because lay Tibetans like to commission monks to perform rites for them.

In Dharmsala, I began to realize what it must mean to be a refugee who had lost everything and lived in exile, far from one's beloved homeland. Take the case of the General: He was a slender, erect, distinguished gentleman, clearly living in straitened circumstances, but treated with the deepest respect by the Tibetan community. I learned that in 1959 he had been in charge of the Dalai Lama's bodyguard. As the invading Chinese closed in, it was the General's responsibility to get the Dalai Lama to safety. Secrecy was crucial, so he could do nothing to get his family out of Tibet; in fact, when he left them for the last time he couldn't even let them know anything out of the ordinary was happening. He succeeded in his mission, but it was at the cost of everything he held dear. Some years later he married another Tibetan lady, and it was in her cafe that we used to meet.

It's one thing to make field recordings of beautiful music, quite another to make these recordings available to a broad audience. In my case, I had the good fortune to meet Teresa Sterne, then the head of Nonesuch Records, when I returned to New York after my first trip to Bali. I played her my field recordings and soon, to my considerable surprise, I had a record, *Music from the Morning of the World*, in Nonesuch's Explorer Series.

So began a little ritual. When I returned to New York from a collecting trip, I would take a cab from the airport straight to the Nonesuch offices. After a warm welcome, Teresa would demand; "What have you got for me this time?"

Only much later did I realize how extraordinary this relationship was. Very few record company heads have both a commitment to world music and the artistic taste to choose wisely. During her fifteen-year tenure at Nonesuch, Teresa created an exceptionally varied and listenable collection of more than 80 records of world music.

Our tastes in world music were remarkably similar. When we listened to my field recordings, we rarely disagreed on musical choices. The chordal chanting of Gyütö Tantric College, a Tibetan monastery, was a good example. (*Listen to disc/tape 1, track 19*)

At that time (1973) most record company executives assumed that Westerners couldn't respond to these rituals. Consequently the few records that were then available contained extremely brief excerpts, treating the chanting as a mere musicological curiosity. Having experienced these rituals at their source, I was well aware of their power, and I urged Tracey to immerse herself in them. She did so, and we came to the same conclusion, namely, that it was impossible to get into the mind-frame of the chanting to brief excerpts. So she agreed to something that was unheard of at the time, a record consisting of two uninterrupted segments of this chanting, each running the full duration of an LP side (twenty-plus minutes). But when I went into the remix studio I pulled a fast one; I laid down not one but two LPs of the Gyütö chanting, each devoted to a particular ritual.

Afterwards I went into Tracey's office and told her what I'd done. There was a pregnant silence, then she said, "I suppose that's a *fait accompli*, isn't it?" And so the two *Tantras of Gyütö* records came into existence, which have enriched the lives of so many people.

Which brings us to the present program. Today, much of what is thought of as world music is better described as "world beat," for it brings together musical elements and instruments from very different cultures; the result is a musical synthesis. For me, world music is very different, it is the vibrant expression of a distinct culture. *Voices of Forgotten Worlds* presents a powerful collection of these unique musical expressions. I hope it gives you as much joy as it has given those of us who collect the music.

David Lewiston lives on the island of Maui. He continues to collaborate with the great Tibetan monasteries in India, recording and documenting their rituals, and he is also working on a series of films of world music and dance. Recently, Lewiston ventured for the first time to the other side of the microphone to make recordings of the Gurdjieff piano music.

TUVANS

"This music is our soul music. It is natural for us to sing. Two out of every three Tuvans can sing this way. In the past, everyone could sing this way. People did it for themselves, when herding sheep."

TUVAN SINGER

It's a hot, sticky summer day in New York. At the Winter Garden plaza of the World Financial Center, a crowd gathers for a performance by a group of Tuvan throat-singers. The musicians warm up and perform a sound-check clad in T-shirts and shorts as microphones are adjusted. A drone is heard from a lone singer, while a whistle-like high-pitched melody, which seems to have no source, hovers above. More and more passersby are drawn toward the curious sounds. As technicians continue to prepare the equipment, two singers in duet create the sound of an entire chorus, covering an immense vocal range.

Ready to perform, the group reenters, this time wearing traditional outfits of brown and bright red, some trimmed in fur. Several have on fur hats. By now a large crowd has assembled. With stringed instruments and hand percussion, the ensemble establishes a simple rhythm, reminiscent of the folk music of many areas. When the singing begins, two, three, even four sounds emanate from an individual singer, ranging from deep growls to high, flute-like tones. In combination with one another, the singers create an almost otherworldly effect. The audience, mostly curious

Americans, sits in rapt attention wearing looks of wonder. The Tuvans onstage grin.

A stone-and-iron monument in Kyzyl, Tuva, on the banks of the Yensei River, has a carved inscription that reads "Center of Asia" in English, Russian and Tuvan, a Turkic tongue. In this territory just north of the border between Russia and Mongolia, the Tuvans, a South Siberian Turkic people numbering some 200,000, make their home.

The most striking music in Tuva is what Tuvans call *khoomei*, in reference to the Mongolian word for "throat." Commonly defined as "throat-singing," Western musicians and ethnomusicologists have also referred to this style as overtone singing, harmonic singing and biphonic or diphonic singing. A single vocalist produces two, even three or four distinct notes simultaneously. This is accomplished by separating and manipulating the voice's natural harmonic overtones, which we typically hear as "color" but not as individual tones. By precisely moving the jaw, curling the lips and manipulating the throat, a Tuvan singer can selectively amplify one or more of the voice's harmonics, and create several melodies at once.

"In 99% of the world, the overtones naturally present in a human voice are ignored. But in Tuva, an isolated land wedged between Siberia and Mongolia, overtones are treasured; they are seen as an expression of one's feelings about nature. Overtones are nurtured, not lost through lack of use.

"For the rest of us, bringing out the overtones in our own voices is next to impossible, something like trying to learn an obscure foreign language with few native speakers available to help us get it right. Nevertheless, we can hear the overtones in a Tuvan's voice."

RALPH LEIGHTON
founder, Friends of Tuva

Ruled by the Mongols and then the Chinese, the Tuvan people formed an independent republic, Tanna Tuva, in 1921 with support

TUVANS

"OUR GRANDFATHERS TAUGHT US TO SING IN THIS
STYLE. NOW, WE ARE TEACHING THE YOUNG PEOPLE
BECAUSE NOT EVERYONE HAS A GRANDFATHER,
AND NOT EVERYONE'S GRANDFATHER CAN SING."

TUVAN SINGER

from the Soviet Union. In 1944, Tuva became part of the USSR. It is now an autonomous republic within the Russian Federation.

"My songs are about my home-land, the high mountains and the streams that run through them. I try to create the sounds of flowing rivers, the sounds of birds and the sounds of animals."

GENNADI T. CHASH
Tuvan singer

Surrounded for the most part by mountains, Tuva was difficult to access until very recently. The first attempt to write down the language of Tuva was made around 1930; before that, culture was carried only through oral tradition. On this almost entirely rural land, the traditional occupation is still herding. Tuvan shepherds perpetuate their age-old nomadic lifestyle, moving often to accommodate their herds.

Most Tuvans form their philosophy and outlook through a lifelong contact with nature and animals. *Steppe kargiraa* ~ a type of throat-singing ~ is sung at the edge of a windblown steppe, the singer turning his head at just the right angle to the wind while carefully shaping his lips

The jew's harp ~ or "mouth harp" ~ is popular throughout Tuva. This small, inexpensive instrument is commonly found among nomadic cultures. In the hands of a Tuvan master, the jew's harp is transformed into a human voice, while in throat-singing, the voice may sound like a jew's harp. Some believe throat-singing to have served traditionally as a means of responding to heightened states of feeling brought on by exaltation at the beauty of the surrounding landscape. Others connect throat-singing to shamanistic ritual.

DISC 1
TRACK. 1
A comic refrain,
"Tuva Kozhangar,"
is performed by the
ensemble "Tuva,"
from the city of Kyzyl.

AINU

The Ainu people, whose name means simply "man," originally inhabited the Hokkaido, Sakhalin and Kurile islands. When the latter two were taken by the Soviet Union after World War II, many Ainu emmigrated to Hokkaido, the northernmost island of Japan, where most live today. The origins of the Ainu are unclear. Their culture and physical appearance is, even today, markedly different than that of the neighboring Japanese.

The Ainu were basically a hunting-gathering population, in stark contrast to the Japanese, Koreans and Chinese, who had been agriculturists for several millennia. Ainu men fished and hunted sea and land mammals, while women were responsible for gathering plants and storing food for the cold season.

In the late 19th century, the Japanese government established complete control over the Ainu, and Ainu society underwent radical change. The Meiji government issued the Hokkaido Aboriginal Protection Act. This legislation required Ainu to attend Japanese schools established by the government. The Ainu were granted plots of land and encouraged to take up agriculture. The tribal system and many of their traditions virtually collapsed. The Ainu language, music and dance were kept alive by only a small number of elders.

"In Japan, not much is known about the Ainu people. There is a great deal of prejudice against them. In the past year, with an increased focus worldwide on indigenous rights, a few Ainu representatives have presented speeches at the United Nations. This has caused the Ainu to feel empowered. The Ainu are ambitious, but perhaps naive in their goals. They want to rewrite the laws, and to declare the Kurile Islands a sovereign nation."

KAREN MICHEL
an independent American radio producer

"WHEN I WAS A CHILD, I WANTED TO SING AN OLD SONG. I LEARNED AN AINU SONG FROM MY GRANDMOTHER. ALL MY FRIENDS GATHERED TO HEAR ME SING THE SONG."

NAKAMOTO MATSUKO
Ainu woman living in Hokkaido

AINU PEOPLE TRANSMIT ORAL HISTORY THROUGH RITUAL SONG.

"MY GRANDMOTHER HAS AN AINU NAME. MY MOTHER AND I DON'T. WE CAN'T HAVE AINU NAMES BECAUSE THE GOVERNMENT WANTS ALL OF THE PEOPLE TO BE JAPANESE. ASSIMILATION POLICY MEANT THAT WE CANNOT SPEAK AINU. THIS POLICY WAS IN PLACE ALMOST ONE HUNDRED YEARS BEFORE I WAS BORN."

NAKAMOTO MATSUKO

AINU WOMEN TRADITIONALLY TATTOOED THEIR LIPS AS A SIGN OF STATUS.

Ainu religion is a mixture of shamanism and animism. Deities are believed to appear to the Ainu in disguise, often in the form of animals. For example, a bear, worshiped above all animals, is seen as the mountain deity bringing gifts of meat and hide.

In Ainu life, religion pervades almost all activities. Even the disposal of leftover food and broken objects is guided by religious and cosmological principles.

Although the Ainu express their religious beliefs in daily ritual, they are best articulated through their oral tradition, which contains many genres. Epic or lyric verses are sung or chanted, and narrative prose is recited. Epics relate the activities of deities, or of cultural heroes, who fought to establish the culture.

Most songs carry melodies that consist of only two or three different notes. Many include mimicry of animal cries and birds singing. Songs are named in reference to their mode of presentation. For instance, there are "sitting songs," "dancing songs," and "pounding songs," sung while preparing flour for dumplings.

DISC 1
TRACK 2
This "*Sitting Song*" is performed by Nakamoto Matsuko, while sitting on the couch in her former cafe, which is still her home in Rankoshi, Hokkaido

TRACK 3
"*Ayoro Kotan*" tells of a beautiful garden village in which the deities gather at night.

Both tracks were recorded by Karen Michel in 1993.

GARIFUNA

The Garifuna people represent a curious mixture of two worlds brought together by shared experience and common circumstance.

I originally went to Guatemala in 1955 to work with the highland Indians but became enamored of the easygoing Caribs. No one seemed to know much except that they were supposedly cannibals. I was driven to continue the search for the roots of these people, who, by the 1970s, were insisting upon their more proper name of Garifuna ~ a modification of the name Kalinago, by which some of their ancestors were known to Columbus.

excerpt from Nanci L. Gonzalez, "Sojourners of the Caribbean"

Early in the 17th century, slaves being transported by the British and Spanish often escaped or were liberated. Others found unexpected freedom as survivors of shipwrecks. Many of these free Africans settled on the island of St. Vincent. They encountered the Island Caribs, who themselves had been displaced by European settlers. The two distinct peoples, both outcasts of European colonial society, began to merge, giving rise to what the British then referred to as "Black Caribs."

St. Vincent was annexed to Great Britain in 1763. The "Black Caribs" staged several rebellions. It took some twenty years for the British to subdue the rebels. In 1797, most "Black Caribs" were deported to the island of Roatán off the coast of Honduras. Finding that island uninhabitable, many

of those exiled found their way to the mainland, then under Spanish rule.

Today the "Black Caribs," known as *Garifuna*, live primarily along the east coast of Central America, from Belize down to Nicaragua, and on the island of St. Vincent. A single Garifuna village remains on Roatán as well.

The Garifuna people have maintained their language, music and lifestyles, which today are enjoying a resurgence. This renewed sense of identity springs from a fascinating story of rediscovery that brings their cultural migration full circle.

"When I went to Belize in the 1950s and inquired about Garifuna culture, the locals referred constantly to the 'old people' in St. Vincent. When I went to St. Vincent, they sent me to Belize.

"In Belize, they held a big celebration called 'Settlement Day' to commemorate the (mythical) day that the Caribs arrived. The Garifuna in Belize sought out three

elder islanders from St.Vincent. They were brought to Belize, after first making a detour through Disneyland. Once in Belize, they were astonished to see their legendary culture still alive.

"What this did was to reawaken in St.Vincent the idea that they had a goldmine of traditions that had not been lost after all. In St.Vincent, they have revived their culture. What they're doing now is mimicking their descendants in Central America."

NANCI L. GONZALEZ

Garifuna religious beliefs reflect the diverse influences present in their ancestry. In addition to the Christian God, they honor the spirits of their ancestors, as well as supernatural beings, around whom they have complicated rituals.

The Garifuna mark their celebrations, both religious and secular, with music driven by strong, easily identifiable rhythms. Each is associated with a particular dance, performed by men and women whose feet never leave the ground. Movement is in the waist and hips, and dancers gently lean forward on their toes. Normally, one person dances in the middle of a circle, responding directly to the call of the drums.

Garifuna dances are based on specific rhythms. *Punta* is usually performed at fiestas, as well as wakes. *Parranda* is the rhythm of celebration at the many Garifuna street parades.

These rhythms are always played on the most important Garifuna drums, referred to as *garaon*. These drums are made from the hollowed trunks of local mahogany trees, carved into conical barrel shapes, with deerskin covers. Hand-crafted rattles, strung turtle shells and wooden blocks are also used for percussion.

"Being Garifuna makes these people distinct, special. They have preserved a language which is a mixture of African languages, Spanish and English and a musical style all their own."

EDUARDO LLERENAS
producer and musicologist based in Mexico City

DISC 1
TRACK 4
"*Busigan*," recorded by
Enrique Ramírez de
Arellano and Eduardo
Llerenas, is a *parranda*,
whose title means
"Let there be no shame."
It proclaims, "Let's be
Garifuna openly to the
world, and have pride
in our own culture."

QUECHUAN

The Quechuan peoples are united by a language and a culture descended directly from the ancient Incas. They live throughout the Andes, from Colombia to Argentina. Of South America's 12 million Quechua, over three million live in Bolivia.

A landlocked country, Bolivia lies in the heart of the South American continent. Its landscape is marked by diversity of terrain. In the west are the Andes mountains rising on either side of the *Altiplano*, a long, high plateau. These highlands occupy more than a quarter of Bolivia's land and are home to the Quechua.

In contrast to the more thinly populated lowlands, the Altiplano and the high valleys are densely inhabited. More than half the people in this area are referred to as "campesino," meaning "countryman or farmer." Engaged in agriculture or cattle raising, the campesino feel themselves bound to the rich cultural heritage of South America.

The Cerro Rico or "Rich Mountain" of Potosi, Bolivia, is so called for its silver deposits, mined extensively by the Spanish in the 16th and 17th centuries. According to Quechuan legend, an ancient Inca discovered the precious metals inside a cave, only to hear a voice speaking Quechuan that warned, "these riches are not for you, they are destined for those that come from afar." Potosi quickly became a focus of the Spanish Empire. Large numbers of Quechuans were forced to move from the country to mining centers, where they earned little and endured terrible health hazards .

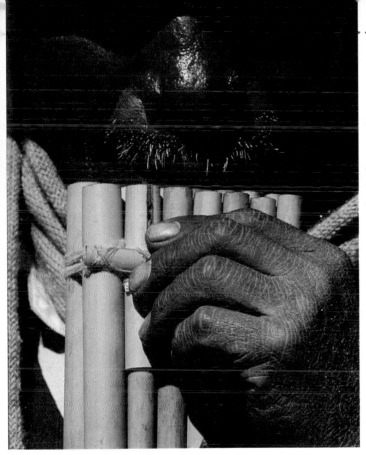

QUECHUAN MUSICAL ENSEMBLES, CALLED "TROPAS," ARE USUALLY MADE UP OF PANPIPES AND FLUTES. PANPIPES CONSIST OF WOODEN TUBES OF DIFFERENT LENGTHS, JOINED TOGETHER IN ROWS. SOME OF THE TUBES ARE CLOSED AT ONE END AND OTHERS OPEN TO PRODUCE TONES OF VARYING PITCHES WHEN PLAYED IN A FLUTE-LIKE STYLE.

After centuries of Spanish rule, Bolivia freed itself and became an independent state in 1825.

The effect of missionary activity was strong, and Roman Catholicism was declared the state religion in the Constitution of 1880. Still, traditional beliefs exist in full vigor even to this day. The campesinos have intermingled their ancient beliefs ~ based around worship of *Pachamama,* the fertility goddess, and *Tio,* the devil or pre-Colombian "Lord of the Hills" ~ with Christian concepts of God and the veneration of Saints.

The many festivals named for the Virgin Mary, for instance, are just as easily associated with the "earth mother." And the cross serves as a traditional symbol for rain and agriculture, in addition to its Christian significance.

Though diminished in number, the campesinos keep alive and vital the festival and celebration rituals that forever intertwine their religion, music and dance.

The Feast of the Assumption of the Blessed Virgin Mary (*Fiesta de la Virgen de Asunción*), marks the beginning of the traditional ceremonies before the planting season, which runs from the end of August into September. This is marked with rituals of sacrifice, masses and processions and music and dance performed in prayer for a good harvest in the coming year.

DURING THE HOLIDAYS, WHICH
OFTEN LAST SEVERAL DAYS AND
CAN CONTINUE FOR MORE THAN
A WEEK, THE PIECES OF MUSIC ARE
PLAYED CONTINUOUSLY FOR
HOURS OR ALL DAY...

excerpt from Max Peter Baumann,
liner notes to "Bolivia: Music in the Andean Highlands"

DISC 1
TRACK 5
"Kantus de Apacheta"
refers to the custom
of building small stone
altars, *apachetas*, at
particular intersections
and pass crossings.
These were constructed
to give thanks, assure
passage and ensure
endurance for journeys.
It is performed at the
*Fiesta de la Virgen del
Carmen*, or Feast of
Our Lady of Mount
Carmel, by a group of
21 musicians playing
panpipes, triangles
and drums. Two pairs
of dancers customarily
perform the accompa-
nying dance, which is
said to have roots in
martial music of the
Inca Guards.

SAAMI

"Each person has his own joik, his own special song. You won't find them collected in any book. They're part of the Saami soul ~ we all carry them. I don't know of any other people with a tradition like this. That's why the joik is irreplaceable to the Saami people."

MATHIS M. GAUP
Saami singer

The Saami people occupy the largest uninterrupted stretch of natural countryside in Europe, from Russia's Kola peninsula down through the mountains of Scandinavia. Their population, estimated at 50,000, is spread across Norway, Finland, Sweden and parts of the former Soviet Union.

Many Westerners refer to these people as *Lapps* and their home as *Lapland*. Saami is the name they prefer; it means simply "man," whereas "Lapp" translates to "people who have been driven to the end of the world."

Traditionally, the anchor of Saami lifestyle has been reindeer herding. Government restrictions and economic forces have threatened this livelihood, altering forever the Saami's relationship with their land and its reindeer.

The Swedish and Norwegian governments control the Saami's rights to own and breed reindeer. Herd limits have been established. Population pressures, industrial development and the exploitation of land and mineral resources have further encroached on the Saami's grazing lands. Reindeer, which provided not only meat and milk but also

materials for garments and tools, are today handled more as a cash crop.

The traditional and modern worlds are juxtaposed throughout Saami life. Reindeer herding is now conducted with the aid of snowmobiles, walkie-talkies and even helicopters. Traditional Saami dress, with its characteristic red embroidery, can be seen on grazing lands or behind the wheel of a Volvo.

The past century has brought a sense of alienation for the Saami. Large groups have been forcibly relocated by Scandinavian governments, and for a long time Saami children received inferior schooling. Authorities, especially in Norway, have pursued a rigorous policy of assimilation.

"At home, talk is all about reindeer and mountain life, and at school, everything is books and modern Norwegian society."
SAAMI STUDENT

Angry protests erupted in Norway during the late 1970s and early '80s, reflecting a new awareness of Saami culture throughout Scandinavia. The activists among the Saami people continue to call for separate treatment. They embrace development, but as Saami, not as Norwegians, Swedes or Finns. Land is a key issue in these confrontations. The Saami have become embattled in the face of the combined pressures of the construction of power stations, dams and parks, growing restrictions on reindeer herding, and the environmental effects of the Chernobyl nuclear disaster.

It is only in the last hundred years that the Saami language has developed a written form. Most of the traditional culture remains known to only a few elders.

The Saami song, or *joik*, has been characterized by a number of researchers as one of the most ancient musical traditions in Europe. A personal joik is a Saami individual's acoustic symbol, shared with a narrow circle of people.

"You learn to joik when you're a small child. Parents can give a joik to their child. When you grow up, it can change. You can give a joik to your sweetheart. Then it's almost the same as an engagement present. It's a gift, one that lasts forever."

ELEN INGA EIRA SARA
Saami singer

DISC 1
TRACKS 6 & 7
Two traditional
Saami joiks.
"Máhte Lemet Elle"
is sung by
Ole Larse Gaino.

"Migal Elle Gáren"
is sung by
Elen Inga Eira Sara.

BUNUN

The Bunun, whose name means simply "person," were the last of the aboriginal cultures in Taiwan to resist Japanese domination. In 1931, independent Bunun tried to defend themselves with bows and arrows, but were subdued by Japanese military planes armed with machine guns.

After World War II, the Chinese National Government pursued a policy of assimilation. A great number of Chinese people moved into tribal areas.

The Bunun are a genuine hill tribe, inhabiting large parts of the central mountain area of Taiwan. There are few written documents tracing Bunun history, as most Bunun rely on oral tradition. That tradition figures in the elaborate and complex Bunun clan system. Each clan is identified by a unique origin myth describing the birth order of their ancestors.

Due to an influx of missionaries in the 1950s, most Bunun, and many Taiwanese in general, are today professed Christians. But the Bunun have adopted an eclectic approach to the religion, retaining the shamanistic beliefs they have held for hundreds of years

Traditionally, the Bunun had an extraordinarily tight schedule of seasonal festivals and rituals that were of immense cultural importance. These were designated with pictures and other marks on wooden boards, festival calendars kept by leaders of the various cult groups. Each year brought well over 100 celebrations, many of them associated with cultivation and harvesting of millet. Today, most of these ritual activities have been abandoned in favor of Christian holidays.

MILLET FARMING IS THE BASIS OF BUNUN LIVELIHOOD.

The Bunun retain their concept of *hanido* ~ the spirit of any animate creature or inanimate object. The hanido spirit leaves and is transformed or disappears when a living being dies or an object vanishes.

"A missionary I worked with suggested I go to Taiwan. He told me I should go quickly, because the music is vanishing."

Dr. Wolfgang Laade
Music of Man Archive, who has recorded the aboriginal tribes of Taiwan extensively

The traditional music of all Taiwanese aboriginal tribes is predominantly vocal, ranging from everyday work-songs to those associated with social and religious activities. Solo singing may introduce a piece, but almost all singing is done in a communal, choral style.

There are songs to make the millet grow, to bless the weapons before a hunt and to celebrate a successful head-hunt (a tradition that has been abandoned). Other songs are more informal. Drinking songs, consisting of meaningless syllables, are sung to celebrate the wine. "Consolation songs," tender choral pieces, dispel feelings of sorrow and "encourage each other to do our best." Oddly, the tune used for one song can be easily adapted to another. For instance, a drinking song and consolation song often bear the same melody.

The jew's harp, made of bamboo and metal, is the most prominent instrument in the music of the Bunun. Tall banana leaves or bunches of long grass are rhythmically shaken to the incantations of healers or shamans, and rattles made from the shoulder bones of wild boar are used by female doctors.

"I don't know when the first 'Aboriginal Culture Village' was created. The fact that the existing ones are strategically located near tourist spots is one indication of their function. In these government-sponsored culture villages, the items are correct, but the context is wrong. The Bunun are singing the same songs wherever they appear. There is now a standard repertoire, and it is certainly drawn from traditional material. I wonder what has happened to the rest of their music."

DR. WOLFGANG LAADE

DISC 1
TRACK 8
"Bisitaita" is a Bunun
song of consolation
which says, "May we
live in peace and
tranquility, without
sorrow and grief..."
It was recorded by
Wolfgang Laade
in the field in 1988.

37

KANAK

The earliest ancestors of the Kanak people came to the islands of New Caledonia from southeast Asia more than 5,000 years ago. The Kanak are the indigenous inhabitants of these islands, an archipelago in the southwest Pacific made up of "Grand Terre," one large island, and a group of smaller islands, referred to as the "Loyalty Islands." The Kanak today make up nearly half of the New Caledonian population.

European and American whalers, merchants and missionaries established regular contact with New Caledonia in the mid-19th century. New Caledonia was annexed by France in 1853, and tribal lands were used for the establishment of a penal colony, settler colonization and nickel mining. Kanak clan territories were systematically reduced. Eventually, Kanaks were confined to native reserves and placed into forced labor. Colonial policy was relaxed after World War II, forced labor eliminated and Kanaks were granted the right to vote.

In 1984, the Kanaks boycotted territorial elections, demanding freedom and "Kanak socialist independence." Violent protests erupted, and in 1988, the Matignon Accords were negotiated between Kanak tribal chiefs, settlers and the French government. The accord imposed a ten year "peace period" during which the French will address Kanak grievances. In 1998, New Caledonians will be asked to choose between independence and staying within the French republic.

RHYTHM IS THE ESSENTIAL ELEMENT OF KANAK DANCE. PICTURED IS A MUSICIAN FROM DUVEA, NEW CALEDONIA.

"When the French settlers came here, they pushed us under the mountains. We were forced to live on reserves the French established.

"In 1988, our leaders signed accords with the French government to strike a balance, but it was not enough. Right now, Kanak children have no chance to get good jobs or take part in the responsibility for administration of government. It is not enough to be granted our land back. We have to work hard for economic development. "There are so many examples of countries in the Pacific who did not develop economically. They have to ask for so many things. The birth of our country is tied to economic development."

NICOLE WAIA
Kanak radio producer

The Kanak people are farmers first and foremost. Fish and game serve as complements to garden produce in their cooking. Traditionally, yams provided the staple diet, and they remain the basis of many religious ceremonial exchanges. However, today, coffee growing for export, mining and industry have replaced subsistence farming.

Kanak music is performed mainly in traditional ceremonial contexts. This communal music, a focus of Kanak social life, takes the form of rhythmic speeches and dances. The two most significant settings are at mourning ceremonies and at a large festival for the first yam of each season. Kanak music is usually sung, with percussion provided by handclaps and stamping feet. Kanak myth holds that two birds taught the people the art of dance, and that the different rhythms were learned from the sounds of rivers and breaking ocean waves.

At their ceremonies, the Kanaks, typically a slow-paced peasant people, begin with exacting protocol and long speeches; these soon give way to abrupt outbursts and wild festivities.

"Our traditions have not changed. It is the mentality of the younger Kanak which has changed. As for the older Kanak, we have our own music, dances and costumes. But the new generation grows up under the French society. If we are not careful, they will lose their dances."

NICOLE WAIA

DISC 1
TRACK 9
"Danse de Toka Nod" was recorded in 1986, at the inauguration of a church on Tiga, the smallest of the New Caledonian Islands. Performed by women wearing garters with rattles. The singers, both men and women, play "leaf drums," small bundles of leaves struck with their hands.

AUSTRALIAN ABORIGINES

Aboriginal Creation myths tell of legendary totemic beings who wandered over the Australian continent in the "Dreamtime," singing out the name of everything that crossed their path ~ birds, animals, plants, rocks ~ in a sense, singing the world into existence.

This labyrinth of invisible pathways is believed by Aborigines to meander all over Australia. Known to Europeans as "Dreaming Tracks" or "Songlines," to the Australian Aboriginal people, they are "the footprints of the ancestors" or "way of the law," the core of an intricate connection between everyday life, ancestry and natural surroundings. They serve as the key to an existence that fuses the everyday with the timeless, the ordinary world with the spiritual world.

"A song," he said, "was both map and direction-finder. Providing you know the song, you could always find your way across the country."

"And would a man on 'walkabout' always be traveling down one of the Songlines?"

"In the old days, yes," he agreed. "Nowadays, they go by train or car."

"Suppose the man strayed from his Songline?"

"He was trespassing ~ he might get speared for it."

"But as long as he stuck to the track he'd always find people who shared his dreaming? Who were his brothers?"

"Yes."

excerpt from Bruce Chatwin, "The Songlines," in which a Russian traveler describes Aboriginal beliefs to the author

The Aboriginal tribes of Australia, traditionally hunter-gatherers, have lived in Australia for thousands of years. Their existence was largely a migratory one, with few material trappings. Their solitary lifestyle, deeply entrenched in a symbolic relationship with the island continent they called home, changed abruptly upon the arrival of European settlers in the 18th century.

White settlers began a long period of violent confrontation, killing many Aborigines and displacing others from their land. The Aboriginal population dropped from an estimated 300,000 at the time of European arrival to under 50,000 by the mid-20th century. Those who survived saw their ancestral lands seized for settlement, a large penal colony, industrial development, and mining; to the Aborigines, this severing of roots and desecration of sacred lands equaled spiritual death.

More recently, Aborigines were forced to learn and speak English, and many were confined to government reserves. They were denied Australian citizenship until 1967. Stories of Aboriginal children removed to be raised in white households

were common. Only in the last two decades has the Australian government begun to address issues of land rights, returning some areas to the Aborigines.

The many Aborigines who now live in cities and villages of Australia are subject to discrimination and what many Aborigines feel amounts to government-sanctioned persecution. Police make one million arrests of Aborigines each year, a number equal to four times the total Aboriginal population.

Music is the most highly prized artistic property, and a powerful force in Aboriginal

43

society. The songman is of great importance. He is seen as "owner" of his "dreamed" songs. Traditionally, a songman controls performances and directs the dancer and musicians.

> "MY MOTHER IS ABORIGINE. SHE NEVER SPOKE HER NATIVE LANGUAGE WHEN I WAS GROWING UP. SHE WASN'T ALLOWED TO. I ONLY LEARNED THIS MUSIC WHEN I TOOK UP DANCE AT AGE 19. WE DIDN'T LEARN ABOUT ABORIGINES IN SCHOOL."

The *didjeridoo,* the traditional musical instrument of the Australian Aborigines, is made from the limb of a eucalyptus tree that has been naturally hollowed out by termites to form a long tube. Though crude in appearance, the didjeridoo can produce a complex variety of drones, overtones, squawks and squeals. Many Aboriginal men learn to play the instrument, but virtuosos are few and are greatly admired. Their songs consist of elaborately encoded information, complicated historical references and intricate rhythmic patterns.

> *"Not a lot of Australians have actually heard a didjeridoo. Only in recent years has it been considered relevant. My own music combines traditional forms with modern influences. I've even developed a hybrid instrument that combines didjeridoo with the slide of a trombone. When I toured in the Northern area, I was concerned that the elders would not approve. But they loved it, and they encouraged me to take it as far as I could."*
>
> ADRIAN ROSS
> *Aboriginal musician and educator*

The highlight of Aboriginal festivity is the *corroboree,* an event where people from neighboring tribes come together to sing and dance their "dreamings" or "songlines." Lasting for several days, these events carry a spiritual significance connected to the region in which they are performed.

DISC 1
TRACK 10
"Dalubun," a traditional
love song, is performed
on didjeridoo and
clapstick with voice.
These songs are used
in Aboriginal weddings,
which typically involve
the entire community.

PASHTUN

In the musical life of Afghanis, men and women play distinctly different roles. In most cases, women do not play or even handle musical instruments other than the tambourine and the jew's harp. Men, however, master many different instruments, including a variety of lutes and fiddles, and they generally shun those instruments favored by women.

> "Pashtun love to listen to music, but as a caste, musicians are associated with vulgarity."
>
> S. SHPOON
> correspondent, "Voice of America"

Situated at the crossroads of eastern and western Asia, Afghanistan emerged in the 19th century as a land of many peoples. It represents the juncture of three major regions: Central Asia, the Near East and India. Each has had a significant influence in Afghanistan at various points in history.

Pashtuns are the largest ethnic group in Afghanistan, making up about half the country's population. Though some Pashtun are nomadic and others urban, the majority live in modest villages.

Traditionally, Pashtun have a negative attitude toward the performing arts. Although this is beginning to wane, individuals still often hide their interest in music and dance to appear "respectable." Dance is especially criticized, as it is seen as evidence of moral laxity.

Despite these restrictive attitudes, folklore and music serve as an important unifying element for the diverse Pashtun groups. Epics and tales abound. One of the tests of a Pashtun musician is his ability to learn and improvise stories and verses based on these epics.

"WE SING MOSTLY NOMADIC SONGS WITH TWO-LINE VERSES, SOMEWHAT SIMILAR TO HAIKU, BUT WITH MORE MEAT."

S. SHPOON

AT THE MEN'S DANCE, "ATAN," PASHTUN MUSICIANS PLAY THE "DHOL," A LARGE, DOUBLE-HEADED DRUM BEATEN WITH STICKS.

"In Pashtun culture, the power of the word is most respected. Poetry is considered high art, music low art. The idea of professional musicians bearing a tradition that is strictly entertainment is not as valued as the art of amateur singers who concentrate not so much on music, but on poetry."

LORRAINE SAKATA
Professor of Music,
University of Washington, Seattle

In Afghanistan as elsewhere, the advent of modern communication has changed the musical landscape. People in northern Afghanistan listen avidly to *Radio Dushanbe* and *Radio Tashkent*. Indian film music is popular in tea houses from Jalalabad to Herat, and Afghani pop music is broadcast by *Radio Afghanistan*. Yet, despite this diversity of outside influences, many ethnic musical styles in Afghanistan remain relatively pure. Such is the case with the *landay*, and several other traditional song forms of the Pashtun.

A landay is a musical form constructed with a nine-syllable verse followed by a thirteen-syllable verse. Performances usually involve a string of landays sung to a single melody. Most landays are composed by women, yet sung by men, a musical phenomenon uncommon among other ethnic groups in Afghanistan.

The most commonly used instrument among Pashtun is the *robab*, a plucked, short-necked lute made of mulberry wood, and featuring three main and fourteen sympathetic strings. The typical Pashtun ensemble combines a robab with a small reed organ called a harmonium, and tabla for percussion.

DISC 1
TRACK 11
"Pashtu Ghazal" is a love poem. This ghazal features a vocal and *robab* duo. It was recorded by Lorraine Sakata in Bakhtu, Afghanistan in 1971.

NEWAR

Forty miles north of the Katmandu Valley in central Nepal, Himalayan peaks rise more than 23,000 feet into the sky. Newar tradition holds that the valley was a deep lake until the god of learning swung his mighty sword to create a huge cleft in the mountains ~ the Chobhar Gorge. Geology bears this out; once, the valley *was* a lake.

Descendants of the Mongol peoples, the Newar are believed to be the original inhabitants of the Katmandu Valley, which has since become home to many other groups. Newar live today mostly in urban clusters set amid agricultural fields. Although they number almost half a million, they are a small minority in Nepal, a country of almost 20 million people, speaking more than 25 languages.

People around the world are familiar with Nepal's tireless Sherpa mountaineers and knife-wielding Gurkha warriors, but they hear little about the Newar, whose sophisticated culture is tucked away amid the Himalayas.

Despite losing their independence two centuries ago, the Newar have clung to their cultural identity, their language, and a complicated set of rituals that reflect an amalgam of Hinduism, Buddhism and animism. The Hindu influence, derived from a group of 14th century Indian Brahmans, brought with it an extraordinarily complex social structure of occupational castes. This rigid caste system governs almost all aspects of Newar life. For instance, because no one can eat food prepared by someone in a caste lower than their own, cooks must be members of a high caste.

This caste system is reflected in musical contexts as well. Ceremonial music is performed by specific ensembles whose instrumentation is determined by the caste to which the musicians belong.

"My whole family would get together and play, and in Nepal that was perfectly natural. All Newar learn how to sing. It is our way of gathering together."
BUDDHA LAXMI SHAKYA
Newar musician

One of the lowest Newar castes, the *Jogi* or *Kusle*, are tailors who are permitted to perform their music only at festivals. The *hāhāh* horn is played only by *Kusah*, who are weavers; the tambourine and cymbals by *Nāy*, who are butchers. *Jyāpu* farmers, the most numerous caste, perform at ritual functions in flute ensembles.

Most Newar music is ritualistic, marking a turning point in one's life, or a seasonal

event. Each ritual ceremony is carefully planned, and must be properly performed. One's safe passage to the afterlife is based not only on an individual's lifetime, but also upon mourners' adherence to burial rituals.

THE FESTIVAL OF SHIKALI, HELD ONLY ONCE EVERY 12 YEARS, IS SAID TO BE SO IMPORTANT THAT NEWAR ARE INTERROGATED BY A GODDESS AFTER DEATH TO MAKE SURE THEY HAVE ATTENDED AT LEAST ONCE.

DISC 1
TRACK 12
"Mārsī-Mālāsri"
combines two compositions, performed by a group of Newar musicians from the *Jyāpu* caste on flutes, drums and cymbals. Typically, this song is associated with a celebration involving sacrifices, feasts and a procession attended by the Valley's entire population.

INUIT

ICEBERGS, DISKO BAY
WEST COAST,
GREENLAND

High atop a hill overlooking a partially-frozen sea, an elderly Inuit man beats a small, simple round drum with a wooden stick. He begins to sing a melodic chant over the beat as he turns his body left, and then right. Bending at the knees, he springs up again and again, moving the drum side-to-side, completely absorbed in his drum-song.

Over 100,000 Inuit people (formerly known as Eskimos) inhabit Greenland, Northern Canada, Alaska and parts of Siberia. *Inngerutit*, their drum-song tradition, was once an integral part of their lives. Not only did Inuit people sing at feasts, they sang every day ~ when they were out sealing, when they were at home, when they felt sorrow, anger or joy. Some songs told elaborate stories, some were more matter-of-fact, others were simple repetitive chants.

"When Christian culture took hold in Greenland, traditional music was basically forbidden. It was looked upon as the work of the devil."

MALIK HOEGH
Inuit recording engineer & producer

Greenland is an intimidating piece of geography, a largely frozen mass whose glaciers constantly feed icebergs into the ragged fjords that fringe its coast. On this forbidding landscape, the Inuit people have been hunters and fishermen for thousands of years. Wind, weather and cycles of animal life directed their activities, and permanent settlements were few. Moving about as animals and nature dictated, Inuit made their homes everywhere and nowhere at the same time, their respect for the land reinforced daily.

This lifestyle continued into the twentieth century, when Greenland came under Danish colonial rule. But forces of modernization sparked by the Danish, a boom in the mining of the region's resources, and the effects of anti-sealing legislation radically altered the Inuit lifestyle and economy. Of the more than 40,000 Inuit ~ who make up a strong majority in Greenland ~ fewer than 1,000 still make their living from hunting. In a land suddenly dotted with neatly trimmed Danish style houses, the Inuit found themselves uprooted and central-ized in communities; many went on welfare.

The crisis of spirit that followed led younger, educated Inuit to voice their demands in the 1970s and, in 1979, Denmark granted home rule. *Kalallit Nunaat*, as Greenland is known in the Inuit language, became the first self-govern-ing arctic native state, an inspiration to others.

Although inngerutit is the most emblematic of Inuit musical forms, Inuit tradition includes a wide range of song styles that serve a variety of purposes. *Anarsaatit* express moods and feel-ings, often with beautiful allusions to nature. *Aqaatit* sing of sealing and the hunt. *Mumerit* involve role-playing games. And duel-songs, called *pisit*, place two singers in competition against each other, often to resolve social prob-lems; in the latter cases, the audience decides who wins.

In the old Inuit society, it was quite common for a person to compose one or more songs. The songs were regarded as part of the person's soul and were therefore his personal property for as long as he lived."

MICHAEL HAUSER
Royal Danish Academy of Music

"Music is a very important part of society right now. People in Greenland are feeling more responsible for their society, and part of this is an immense respect for their own culture. Traditional drum-dancing has started again. It is even beginning to be taught in schools."

HJALMAR DAHL
Greenlander working at the U.N. Center for Human Rights

Respect for tradition is central to Inuit music. Songs must be rehearsed carefully and, when performed, they must be sung precisely and in the correct style. Composing freely was inconceivable in traditional Inuit music. Any musical individuality had to be expressed within agreed-upon local styles.

"The state of our society demands that the youth speak and understand both Danish and Greenlandic. It is important that they have a Greenlandic language that is comprehensible and comparable. That's why we need the songs."

MIKI PETERSEN
*excerpt from "Inuusuttut Nipaat 1,"
a book on Inuit music.*

"Things changed with the new movement toward the end of the 1970s. Young people were looking for their identity. In the '50s and '60s, all Inuit in Greenland were required to learn Danish culture. It was very frustrating. I was part of the Aasavik movement, to help restore tradition. We are looking back ~ to the drum and to the kayak. 'Aasavik' means the traditional summer camp. These have been held in different spots each year, beginning in 1976. It is mostly young students. We gather together to discuss our political situation, and at night we play all kinds of music ~ rock music, traditional drumming."

MALIK HOEGH

AN INUIT MAN
DRUM-SINGING IN
THULE, GREENLAND

DISC 1
TRACK 13
"Imína Imína" is a
traditional Inuit song
about the great hunter
by that name, from
Siorapaluk, the
northernmost
settlement in the world.

TRACK 14
"Navssápaluk
Sadorana" is a typical
drum-song, recorded in
1984. Another record-
ing of this song, from
1909, reveals an almost
identical performance
style, 75 years earlier.

MAYA

A tour guide at the legendary ruins of Palenque in Chiapas, Mexico likes to tell the story. A tourist, after staring in awe at the towering pyramids, turned to the guide and said, "The buildings are beautiful, but where did all the people go?" "Of course, she was talking to a Maya," the guide says, shaking his head at the irony. "We're still here. We never left."

excerpt from Guy Garcia,
"Forgotten But Not Gone," in Time magazine

There are more than one million Maya living today in the southern Mexican state of Chiapas. Another nearly 5 million are spread throughout the Yucatan Peninsula and the cities and rural farm communities of Belize, Guatemala, Honduras and El Salvador.

The Mayan civilizations flourished for almost a thousand years, only to disappear abruptly around 900 AD. Maya have been credited with perfecting a complex writing system, and devising precise mathematics and astrological calendars. The massive pyramids they built across Central America serve as both living monuments and tourist destinations. Today, the Maya remain the subject of both popular and academic fascination, as much for their achievements as for their sudden collapse.

In an account of travels from 1839 through 1842, American author John Lloyd Stephens documented his arrival at what was later identified as the ruined Mayan city of Copán:

…unless I am wrong, we have a conclusion far more interesting and wonderful than that of connecting the builders of these cities with the Egyptians or any other people. It is the spectacle of a people skilled in

architecture, sculpture and drawing, and, beyond doubt, other more perishable arts, and possessing the cultivation and refinement attendant upon these, not deriving from the Old World, but originating and growing up here, without models or masters, having a distinct, separate, independent existence; like the plants and fruits of the soil, indigenous.

excerpt from John Lloyd Stevens, "Incidents of Travel in Central America, Chiapas and Yucatan"

In modern history, the Maya have suffered systematic persecution. After the Spanish conquered this area in the 16th century, missionaries outlawed Mayan religion, destroying sacred bark-paper texts. Under Spanish rule, Maya who survived the armed conflict were forced into slavery on colonial plantations. For nearly 400 years Maya have resisted the domination of Spain and later, of Mexico. In a 1992 report, Amnesty International cited dozens of human rights violations carried out against the Maya by Mexican authorities.

For many visitors to Chiapas, their first look at the Maya is of farmers along the highway to San Cristóbal, whose iridescent tunics and beribboned straw hats sparkle in the gray fog that envelopes their fields. From a distance, their settlements, especially the smaller ones, seem bucolic, nestled in the quiet pine forests, with smoke rising from cooking fires and sheep grazing on the hillsides nearby…. These images of pastoral serenity are unreal, of course. The Chiapas highland Maya are starved for land and food.
excerpt from Kevin Gossner, "Soldiers of the Virgin: The Moral Economy of a Colonial Maya Rebellion"

A number of Mayan communities have maintained their traditional ways in the face of modernization. In the remote highlands of Guatemala and Mexico, where the rugged terrain has slowed the encroachment of the outside world, contemporary Maya still live in ways similar to their ancestors 4,000 years ago.

"In December 1975, I took off for some very different mountains, the Chiapas highlands of Southern Mexico. Chiapas is the most Indian state in Mexico, and in the highlands the majority of the people still bear the features of their Mayan ancestors. I was struck by the similarities here with Andean cultures; in both, the Spanish invaders grabbed the fertile lowlands, leaving the original inhabitants with only the much poorer highlands. In both, their descendants preserve ancient traditions.

"In Chiapas, the festivals perpetuate some of these traditions. Music is an essential ingredient of a fiesta. Alcohol is also essential, for drinking is considered religious behavior. The favorite drink is pox, rum; like music, pox is said to be a gift from God to make people happy."

DAVID LEWISTON

"Our ancestors performed this and our children will perform this too. The fiesta goes and the fiesta continues to arrive, never to die and never to be finished."
from a Mayan ceremony

My commitment to our struggle knows no boundaries or limits. This is why I've travelled to many places where I've had the opportunity to talk about my people. Of course, I'd need a lot of time to tell you all about my people, because it's not easy to understand just like that. And I think I've given some idea of that in my account. Nevertheless, I'm still keeping my Indian identity a secret. I'm still keeping secret what I think no one should know. Not even anthropologists or intellectuals, no matter how many books they have, can find out all our secrets.

excerpt from "I, Rigoberta Menchu…
an Indian Woman in Guatemala," an autobiography

AZERBAIJANI

"WHEN HE BEGAN TO PLAY, I FELT FROZEN TO MY SEAT, AS IF A WIND HAD BEEN BLOWING THROUGH ME. I WAS DETERMINED TO LEARN FROM THIS MAN, AND TO PLAY THIS MUSIC."

ZEVULON
AVSHALOMOV
("MR. Z")

"Twenty years ago, I was living in Los Angeles, where I composed music and performed on guitar and piano. Someone who heard me play advised me that if I ever had the opportunity, I should listen to this older guy from a strange part of the world who played strange music.

"I finally located this man, known around town as 'Mr. Z.' He was a self-taught musician from Azerbaijan, about sixty years old. He played the 'kamancha,' a bowed fiddle. Since he spoke no English and I spoke only English, we communicated through his son at first.

"He resisted the idea that he could ever teach a Westerner this music, but I was persistent, and within a few months, I was up and running. I spent a few years as his apprentice, learning all I could.

"I was under the impression that I had learned a dying art. A year later, I met professional musicians from Baku, and I realized this tradition was very much alive and well. We became friends instantly; they were astonished that a Westerner could embrace their culture.

"Finally, I traveled to Azerbaijan. This was just as the Soviet Union was dissolving. When I arrived in Baku, my musician friends drove me from the airport. By this time, I knew some Cyrillic, and I excitedly translated graffiti on a wall that read "Democracy." My friends laughed, asking, 'Do you have 'democracy' written on a wall?'"

JEFFREY WERBOCK
American musician and devotee of Azerbaijani culture

Azerbaijan covers an extensive area of the Caucasus and the northwestern highlands of Iran. In 1828, it was divided: one part was turned into a province of Iran, the other incorporated into the Tsarist Empire, later to become a constituent republic of the Soviet Union. With the collapse of the USSR, Azerbaijan is now an independent republic within the Russian Federation.

Azerbaijan was an ancient homeland to Persian culture. The Turkic traditions of

Central Asia reached this area in the 10th and 12th centuries carried by waves of nomads. After a period of autonomy followed again by Persian rule, the Caucasus was joined to Russia, in 1828, and Azerbaijan was divided. Azerbaijani musical tradition has since taken two different directions, evolving autonomously in the north, but being absorbed by Persian music in Iran.

Azerbaijani music encompasses three major forms: *mugam*, their classical or "art" music; traditional folk songs; and the poetic song tradition of the *ashiq*, who are traveling bards.

In all forms of Azerbaijani music, the most popular instruments are the *kamancha*, a bowed fiddle, the *tar*, a guitar-like lute, and the *saz*, a lute favored by the ashiq. *Bâlâbân*, a double-reeded woodwind was traditionally popular, but it has now been widely replaced by clarinet and accordion.

The mugam, the classical or "art" music of Azerbaijan is largely a meterless form of music. It is a difficult tradition which, once mastered, allows the musician to personalize the themes.

But it is the music of the ashiq bards, who travel from region to region, that serves as a unifying force to perpetuate traditional Azerbaijani music, and transmit stories and epics through an age-old oral tradition.

"Ashiq are special singers. They are like the European bards. In the past, they wore uniforms of the Caucases with bullets on the breasts and a dagger on the belt. Since they were always traveling between the villages and towns, they were seen as always 'being on alert.' During Soviet rule, they were not allowed to wear military uniforms. They wore them anyway but removed the stars and stripes which represent military rankings.

ALI RASIZADE
Fellow in Azerbaijani-American relations at the Kennedy Institute, originally from Azerbaijan

The term "ashiq" derives from the Arabic word meaning "lover." It is said that an incurable heartache pushes the ashiq to seek consolation in singing his woes, in the form of a repertoire of poems praising the beauty of his beloved or of nature. Ashiq bards are required to spend years with one or more teachers, committing to memory famous poems, entire epics and melodic formulas. As they travel from town to town with their saz over their shoulder, the ashiq earn renown not only based on their voice and magnetism, but also on the extent of their repertoire.

DISC 1
TRACK 16
"Koroghlu" is a 16th century poem, which commemorates a folk hero of the same name. It is performed by an *ashiq*, one of the legendary Azerbaijani bards, performing on the *saz* (lute) in a trio with *bālābān* (double-reed woodwind) and *daf* (percussion).

MAORI

According to legend, Maori ancestors launched their canoes to *Aotearoa*, the "Land of the Long White Cloud," better known as New Zealand. Long known as a warrior race, the Maori have been tied to their land ever since with a fierce determination.

European sealers, traders and missionaries arriving in New Zealand in the early 1800s met with violent resistance from the Maoris, who had lived on those lands for centuries. Ongoing skirmishes over land rights persisted for decades. Modern New Zealand was founded with the Treaty of Waitangi in 1840, which marked an agreement between the sovereign chiefs of the Maori people and the British crown on behalf of the European settlers.

Under the treaty, the Maori people relinquished political sovereignty over New Zealand and, in return, received British recognition and protection, as well as guaranteed land rights. Relations deteriorated,

> "I BELIEVE WE SURVIVE BECAUSE OF THE STRENGTH OF OUR CULTURE. WE SURVIVE BECAUSE OUR SPIRITUALITY IS ROOTED IN THE LAND. WE SURVIVE BECAUSE KINDNESS, FORGIVENESS AND GENEROSITY ARE INHERENT IN OUR BELIEFS."
>
> SELWYN MURU
> *a Maori elder who is also a journalist, screenwriter and sculptor*

THE WARRIOR TRADITION OF THE MAORI PEOPLE IS EXPRESSED IN THEIR DANCE

disputes arose over land rights and war broke out in the 1860s. The Maoris were eventually subdued. In the years following, Maori self-determination was replaced by assimilation, which raised the profile of Maoris, but also threatened their culture.

One hundred and fifty years after the signing of the Waitangi Treaty, the Maori, who make up 10 percent of New Zealand's population, still wait for that agreement to evolve into meaningful action. These days, however, Maori activists use nonviolent means to achieve their goals.

"There has been a huge resurgence of Maori culture due to a resurgence of the language. We've organized 'language nests' (called 'khanga reo') which pre-school children go to in order to learn the Maori language. Just about every person in New Zealand has been touched by these language nests in some way. Not everyone who attends is Maori."

TE RANGI HUATA
marketing manager,
Kahurangi Maori Dance Theater of New Zealand

"Forty or fifty years ago, Maori were barred from speaking their language in school. There have been big changes since then ~ so much so that these days, Maori is taught in my daughter's primary school."

TERENCE O'NEILL-JOYCE
producer, living in New Zealand

For the Maori people, music and dance are inseparable. It is through their distinctive musical tradition that the Maori reflect their warrior tradition and their intense spirituality, as well as the influence of European culture.

Traditional Maori music includes "action songs" and chants. Action songs are performed with hand gestures as a form of sign language. *Waiata* and *Haka* are the two traditional styles of chants. Waiata are most commonly used today in welcome ceremonies. Haka are wardances. These derive from battle situations, and were used to literally insult or "scare off" enemies.

After European influence, Maori music bears the mark of Christianity, with songs styled after the melodies of hymns. Contemporary Maori music uses the melodies of Western secular songs, combined with Maori text and harmonies. In all Maori music, the most clearly identifiable features are rich and slightly discordant harmonies drawn from traditional chants, and the athleticism and vibrancy of the accompanying dances.

"In our music, the most important element is the message. Our messages are of spirituality. We don't merely sing of love or of personal feelings.

"Our wardances are one of the most colorful aspects of our music. They are based on insulting the enemy. Opposing armies would stand 200 meters apart and, while they chanted, they would stick their tongues out, roll their eyes, grimace and snarl. This traditional form of dance has been incorporated into our ceremonies today.

"Our music and dance are based on our warrior tradition. That energy is now channeled into our dances. It's much different than European folk dancing. In Europe, the dances have a repetitive style, with circles or pairs. All our dances are based on battle formations."

TE RANGI HUATA

Strong spiritual beliefs and a heritage of violence are not seen as opposing forces by the Maori. This is perhaps best evidenced by the Maori word for enemy, *"hoa riri,"* which means "friends in anger."

For the Maori people, protecting their culture and their land are primary concerns. Music and dance are seen as elemental to these efforts.

DISC 1
TRACK. 17
"He Toa Takitini" and *"Ka Tohia Atu Koe,"* two action songs, are followed by *"Ki Okoiki,"* a traditional *haka,* or wardance. These were recorded by Terence O'Neill-Joyce in New Zealand in 1987.

RASHAIDA

Eritrea, an independent state, is a land of imposing geography. It is dominated by a south-central highland that rises 10,000 feet. To the south are extinct volcanoes and fields of broken lava. To the west are plains, crossed by fertile lowlands. In the east, dropping sharply to the Red Sea is the coastal plain, a narrow strip of barren scrubland and desert.

Long ago, Eritrean lands yielded food; areas once described as forest are now seas of dust. The famine that has hit Eritrea and much of sub-Saharan Africa has been caused largely by drought and erosion. The drought of the 1980s and the subsequent famine throughout Ethiopia brought these conditions to worldwide attention. But for over a decade prior, the land and its resources had also been ravaged by the bloody battles of rebels seeking independence. These battles continued throughout the 1980s.

Recorded history traces Eritrea to the second millennium B.C., when Egyptian Pharaohs conducted trade with Red Sea coastal chiefs. Its highland areas became

THE RASHAIDA
ARE A NOMADIC
PEOPLE WHOSE
TENTS ARE EASILY
MOVED AS THEY
TRAVEL WITH THEIR
CAMEL HERDS.

RASHAIDA WOMEN WEAR COLORFULLY DECORATED TRADITIONAL MASKS CALLED "ARUSI."

part of the kingdom of Axum two thousand years ago. In the fourth century, the Axumite kingdom was converted to Christianity. The region saw invasions by the Turks and Egyptians and, in the early 19th century, became the first of several Italian colonies in Africa. During the period of Italian rule, Eritrea developed rapidly.

Italy lost the colony to British invasion in 1941. After World War II, a United Nations resolution made Eritrea an autonomous,

> **"THE RASHAIDA HAVE THEIR OWN STYLE OF DANCING. IT IS VERY ELEGANT, WITH THE WOMEN WEARING COLORFUL VEILS."**
>
> ELIAS AMARE
> *Communications Director, Eritrean Cultural Civic Center, Washington, D.C.*

self-governing region of Ethiopia. But in 1962, Ethiopia formerly annexed Eritrea, discarding its flag and forcing the adoption of the Ethiopian language, *Amharic*.

The civil wars of the 1970s and '80s finally came to an end in May of 1991, with the defeat of the Ethiopian army. In 1993, after a two-year transition period, Eritreans voted overwhelmingly in favor of independence.

Eritrea's four million inhabitants comprise nine diverse ethnic groups, each with their own culture and music. The new government has a policy of promoting multi-culturalism. Radio stations have time slots allocated for each ethnic group, and each child learns their own ethnic language in school.

The Rashaida are a small Arabic-speaking group of nomads along the northeastern Eritrean desert. Strongly conservative, they are deeply religious Muslims. Rashaida traditionally breed camels in small pastures near oases. As in many of the nomadic cultures of this area, music consists primarily of songs, with handclaps and stamping feet for percussion.

> *"The lifestyle of the Rashaida has changed, as today most of them are traders. Now you see Rashaida driving Landcruisers across the border instead of camels."*
>
> ELIAS AMARE

DISC 1
TRACK 18
"Rashaida Dance"
At the feasts which mark the end of Muslim Ramadan, the Rashaida of Eritrea gather to hold camel races by day, and to sing and dance into the night. At dances, a drummer sits in the center of a huge semicircle of women who dance while men sing and clap.

73

TIBETANS

Tibetan Buddhism, and in relation to the Dalai Lama, a leader who is both devoutly followed and passionately revered.

The 14th Dalai Lama, who Tibetan Buddhist monks believe to be the reincarnation of the Boddhisatva of Compassion, is both spiritual leader and head of state. Chosen for the position as a very young boy, the Dalai Lama assumed his status at the age of five. By 1949, the People's Republic of China was formed, and in 1950, Chinese Communists invaded Tibet. The Dalai Lama, then 17 years old, was forced to flee to India. Though he returned to Tibet for a short time, the Dalai Lama soon fled again. He was welcomed in Dharamsala, India, where he has remained ~ one of the world's most influential spiritual leaders, living in exile for most of his life.

"I set out to visit some noteworthy monasteries nearby. One was Gyütö Tantric College, whose monks use a remarkable chanting style which sounds as though each participant is singing in chords. Word of Gyütö's chanting had already reached the West, and in scholarly journals, musicologists and acousticians analyzed how the sound is created. Apparently, Gyütö's members produce low bass notes with unusually rich overtones, so that it sounds as though each participant is producing a chord. But this dry technical description doesn't begin to convey the timeless deep peace which Gyütö's slow-moving melodies evoke. This kind of chanting is truly ancient."

DAVID LEWISTON

The history, culture and people of Tibet can only be appreciated in the context of

Following the Dalai Lama's departure, full-scale conflict broke out in Tibet. Monasteries were looted, sacred icons and

74

THE DALAI LAMA SITS BEFORE A BUDDHIST MANDALA.

texts destroyed. Over a million Tibetans perished and more than six thousand monasteries were leveled.

The Chinese implemented a series of oppressive economic and political measures. Forced changes in agricultural practices resulted in the first famine in Tibetan history. Mineral deposits seized from Tibet now account for nearly half of China's total mineral wealth. As a result, Tibet has withered to the point of near collapse.

Tibetan culture, however, continues to flourish in pockets around the world. Over 100,000 Tibetans live in exile in India. Another 6 million are scattered through Nepal, Bhutan, Switzerland, England and the United States. The Dalai Lama remains the source of spiritual and political inspiration for this borderless state, as well as to many millions of followers not originally from Tibet. He continues to embody compassion and command respect, and to work for peaceful reconciliation of conflicts in Tibet and throughout the world.

Buddhism, the state religion, was transmitted by a series of Indian teachers who visited Tibet in the 8th Century. The advent of Buddhism was so powerful and lasting that at the time of the Chinese invasion there were about a half million monks living in Tibet, representing 10 to 20 percent of the male population.

Tantra, the highest spiritual path in Tibetan Buddhism, centers around visualizations, hand gestures and the chanting of Buddhist scriptures. Since sound and music play an important religious role, it is not surprising that Tibet's most remarkable music is found in monasteries.

Founded in 1474, Gyütö Tantric College became one Tibet's most prestigious institutions of higher learning. By the 1950s, it had 900 members. Only a monk who had passed through a grueling course of instruction and achieved the status of geshe, doctor of divinity, could join the college. When the Chinese ravaged Tibet in 1959, they destroyed most of Gyütö.

One hundred of Gyütö's members managed to escape to India. The refugees reestablished their college near the hill town of Dalhousie. There, they endured difficult living conditions. The Indian government provided them with rations worth only one *rupee* (then ten cents) per day. In order to support themselves, the monks made carpets for two or three rupees a day. As if this burden were not enough, they also took on the responsibility of raising several small children as novices. The monks and novices have managed to keep alive a tradition thought to be five centuries old.

"One afternoon I set up my recording equipment in the back of the temple as the monks were performing a ritual. Afterwards, Tara Rinpoche, the abbot of Gyütö, came over and asked what I had been doing. I passed him the headphones, and he listened to the recording.

"He was delighted. It was the first time he had heard a good recording of the Gyütö chanting. He told me that the monastery had been looking for someone to record their most important rituals as an archive, and asked whether I could help. Naturally, I was delighted to help.

"Over tea in his office, we discussed how to make a clean recording. It was the monsoon season, and rain made a great deal of noise on the temple's corrugated iron roof, so we agreed that if it began to rain, recording would stop. The other sources of noise, dogs and children, were dealt with by having the young novices drive the dogs away before each recording session, and then keeping the children away as well. Tara Rinpoche and the 'umzes,' leaders of the chanting, carefully selected the monks with the best voices to make the recording."

DAVID LEWISTON

DISC 1
TRACK 19
This track was excerpted from "*Gyütö Tantra*," a recording of chants performed at Gyütö Tantric College made by David Lewiston in 1975.

LADAKHIS

Deep in the Himalayas, at the western edge of the Tibetan plateau is one of the highest and driest inhabited regions in the world. Frozen eight months of the year, this high altitude desert in the Indian state of Jammu and Kashmir features fields surrounded by areas of rock and desert. In this terribly challenging landscape, the people of Ladakh not only survive, they prosper.

The Ladakhi people look Tibetan and share Tibetan Buddhist culture, religion and language. In fact, historically, and even today, the area has been called "Little Tibet." In this barren wilderness, nothing grows wild. By channeling water from snow-fed streams, the Ladakhi have formed oases. One can find crops growing in terraces, hacked from a mountainside around a village or Buddhist monastery.

Over the centuries, the Ladakhis have maintained a delicate balance with their environment. Population, animal herds, natural resources and manpower have been scrupulously managed. Until 1962, Ladakh was almost completely isolated, but due to India's border conflicts with China and Pakistan, a road was built by the Indian army to link the region with the rest of India. Forces of modernization were accelerated when, in 1975, the region was opened to foreigners. The influx of packaged goods and a now-booming tourism industry have changed, even threatened, the Ladakhi way of life.

The greatest gift that the West can give is a more conscious appreciation of what the Ladakhis have had for centuries, because they have something that we have almost lost. The balance with the natural world and the essential harmony in terms of relationships is something we can consciously

appreciate better than the Ladakhis can, because we know what it's like to lose it.

excerpt from an interview in INCONTEXT magazine, with Helena Norberg-Hodge, author, and founder of The Ladakh Project

While the traditional music of Ladakh resembles that of Tibet, a newer style has developed, reflecting Western influences in terms of instrumentation and political themes. Among traditional instruments, the most popular are the *damnyan*, a banjo of sorts with a hide-covered casing, the *surna*, a double-reed wind instrument, and the *limbo*, a transverse flute.

"In summer, the Ladakhis take advantage of the warm weather to throw lots of parties. The first requirement for a party is a nice garden, which is really something special in this arid country. In the garden, musicians play double-reed shawms and drums and everybody dances. There's always a popular local sport, like archery going on. Even the monks join in these diversions.

"Wherever Ladakhis are hard at work— in the fields, carrying loads in the street, building houses - they sing work songs. The leader sings a brief phrase, and the others respond, as simply as, 'Now we are cutting the grain,' or, 'Now this plot is cleared. They exhibit an incredible joy in life."

DAVID LEWISTON

DISC 1
TRACK 19
"Ghungsgot thonpo," or "The High Sky," is a traditional song celebrating the natural beauty of the surroundings. In this recording, made by David Lewiston, a female singer is accompanied by a *damnyan* player.

SOLOMON ISLANDERS

"Much of what the white man brought here was in conflict with our culture. Maybe the natives saw that they couldn't go on living the same way. The white man brought with him many attractions: better tools, clothing, entertainment. But we let go of a lot of good things."

JAN SANGA

a Solomon Islander who now works for the Central Bank of the Solomon Islands

In 1567, a Spanish explorer, Alvaro de Mendana de Neira, discovered a small archipelago in the South Pacific. Formed from the peaks of two chains of submerged mountains, the islands feature some rugged terrain, including several volcanic areas. The treasure of King Solomon was believed to be hidden there. And though no such bounty was ever found, the name Solomon Islands has endured.

After de Neiras' ship departed, there was little European contact with the island for the better part of two centuries. In the mid-1800s, missionaries began to visit the Solomons, and by the end of that century, the islands were under British rule. Many Solomon Islanders were shipped to Fiji or Australia as forced laborers on plantations.

Toward the end of World War II, Guadalcanal, the largest of the Solomon Islands, came to worldwide attention as the site of a pivotal confrontation between U.S. and Japanese forces. It was a defining event in the history of the Solomon Islands.

The Japanese had invaded the Solomon Islands in the early 1940s. In the desperate fighting which followed between the Japanese and Americans, the U.S. forces received strong support from the islanders. Following the Allied victory, the United States established a vast military complex, employing thousands of islanders.

New wealth flooded the island as a result of the presence of the American military. And, though it was mostly the pickings of junk heaps and surplus stores, it was a revelation for the islanders, an indication of the overwhelming material bounty of Western civilization. Things would never be the same.

A growing political consciousness among Solomon Islanders inspired a nationalist movement known as Maasina Rule, lasting from 1944 to 1952. That pressure, along with decolonization of the British Empire, set the islands on the path toward independence, finally attained in 1978.

Unfortunately, because of the changes that have occurred in our people's way of life since the coming of the 'araikwao' (the white man), the value of much traditional knowledge is now less appreciated than it once was…. The learning of the garden must now compete with that of the school, the church, the workplace and the town. As a result our main means of access to what our ancestors knew, and thought, and felt, and did is in danger of being lost.

excerpt from, Jan Sanga, "Solomon Islands: The Past Four Thousand Years"

Songs and dances have traditionally been an essential element of communication on the Solomon Islands. The *rihe mumu*, a panpipe ensemble, is still the most popular musical form. The name derives from *rihe*, panpipes, and *mumu*, the name of mythical savages from whom, according to the oral tradition, the men stole their instruments.

DISC 2
TRACK 1
"Mbumbusa" or
"Warrior's Cry" is a
piece performed by a
rihe mumu, a panpipe
ensemble on the
island of Guadalcanal.
TRACK 2
"Vinango" or
"Voyage by Canoe,"
recorded on the island
of Savo, whose musical
tradition is strictly
vocal. This song is
performed by a *lalaa*,
a traditional chorus of
both men and women.

BA-BENJELLÉ PYGMIES

Alone in a northern European capital one winter night, I turned on the radio ~ and rediscovered music. The song on the air was unlike anything I had ever heard: voices blending into a subtle polyphony, weaving a melody that rose and fell in endless repetition, as hypnotic as waves breaking on a shore. At the end the announcer spoke in Flemish, and all I learned was that the song had come from somewhere in central Africa…. I became obsessed with that song and set about trying to track it down. By the time I did, I had come across several recordings of similar music, and I knew that it was a song of the Pygmies.

excerpt from Louis Sarno, "Song from the Forest"

For Louis Sarno, an American from New Jersey, thus began a strange and wondrous musical odyssey. It ended in a rainforest deep in the Central African Republic, where Sarno met and fell in love with a Pygmy woman, and where he now makes his home among the Ba-Benjellé Pygmies, a clan of the Aka Pygmy tribe.

At first, Sarno was allowed only a partial view of the Pygmies' lifestyle. He supplied endless quantities of cigarettes to the Pygmies, but soon began to question his naive dream of finding an intact, noble and ancient culture. Still Sarno persevered. Living exclusively on the native diet of greens and tadpoles, he gradually gained the respect and friendship of the Pygmies. He was eventually allowed to participate in their hunts and musical ceremonies, where he witnessed the breathtaking phosphorescent body art of the *mokoondi*, the jungle spirits, and fell asleep to the low yodeling of the women as they chanted into the night.

"At the beginning, they showed me what they would perform for, say, a visiting

"THEIR MUSIC, WHICH FEATURES EXQUISITE POLYPHONY, SUBTLE CALLS AND RESPONSES AND DISTINCT HARMONIES, IS A REFLECTION OF THE EGALI-TARIAN NATURE OF THEIR SOCIETY. EVERYONE HAS A PART, BUT ALONE IT'S NOTHING. WHEN THEY COME TOGETHER THEY MAKE THIS BEAUTIFUL WHOLE. THE COLLABORATION THEY HAVE IN THEIR SOCIETY IS NOT FORCED, THEY COOPERATE OUT OF THEIR OWN HEART."
LOUIS SARNO

minister - which usually leaves most people satisfied. But someone who knows what they perform for themselves knows this would require no effort on their part.

"I think they realized I knew they could do better. I think it was the women at first. They made this decision to show me they could sing, that they did have other music. I think they made an educated guess that, maybe, I was genuinely interested in their music and they wanted to show me more than what they usually show outsiders. In exchange, they demanded I give them my life ~ which is what I have done. I think it's a fair exchange."

LOUIS SARNO

Known to most Westerners for their short stature, the Pygmies of central Africa comprise the largest population of hunter-gatherers remaining on earth. Although most other groups in the area fear the forests and remain on its periphery, the Pygmies have made their home amidst its gigantic trees and dense foliage since ancient times.

The name 'Pygmy' dates back to ancient Greece, although Pygmies appear in the historical record long before that time. After Aristotle, however, the Pygmies were considered to be a myth; only in the second half of the 19th century were they "rediscovered" by modern Europe.

The women gathered at one end of the camp and started to sing. Men and boys, many of the latter with hats made out of strips of palm leaf, gave high-pitched cries. At the back of the camp men constantly walked up a path into the forest, curtained off with palm leaves. Soon a chorus of two-note cries approached. The curtain parted and out came each group of men and boys wielding sticks and leafy branches. They surrounded a central figure, tapping it with their sticks, and as the entourage made its way into the clearing I got a closer look. The figure, draped in a mass of raffia fibers, was shaped roughly like a haystack. It neared the women and began to whirl, its raffia dress fanning out. As it whirled it grew in height and moved across the clearing. The women set off in pursuit, dancing

*after it. "Yo!" everyone cried. It leaped up
again. The women retreated, laughing and
shouting. The figure began to dance again.
It was Ejengi.*

excerpt from Louis Sarno, "Song from the Forest"

DISC 2
TRACK 3
This recording of
Ba-Benjellé Pygmies,
made by Louis Sarno,
documents a ceremony
for the forest spirit
Ejengi, the most
famous of all the forest
spirits. An appearance
of the *Ejengi* with his
phosphorescent body
paint commonly leads
to days and days of
dancing and ceremony.

UIGHURS

The Silk Road is a modern collective term for the great overland trade routes that once linked China with the West. Of tremendous importance to the ancient world, it made possible not only the exchange of silk and innumerable other wares, but also the diffusion of cultural ideas and artistic styles. Religion and language passed as readily as textiles and spices among China, Persia, India, Byzantium and even Rome by way of the Silk Road.

In Central Asia, Silk Road traders were forced by geography to pass through the oases of the Tarim Basin, an arid plateau ringed by mountains in what is now known as the Xinjiang region of China. The Uighurs, a dominant Turkic tribe, were one of the original inhabitants of this area, and they imbued it with Turkic influence.

Music seems always to have played an important role along this route. Chinese dynastic annals and the chronicles of travelers over two millennia reinforce a picture of rich cultural life in the oases during the height of Silk Road trade. Buddhist cave murals in these areas reveal a great variety of instruments ~ harps, flutes, drums and most prominently, lutes.

As overland trade gave way to sea routes, the Silk Road gradually disappeared. It had, however, served a great economic and cultural purpose, and had created the foundations of an enduring music tradition.

The present-day Uighur are concentrated in the oasis cities of the Xinjiang region. The name "Uighur" had dropped out of usage after the 15th century, when much of the largely Buddhist population converted to Islam. "Uighur" was revived by the Soviets in the 1930s as a term for those

oasis peoples who, at the time, had no names for themselves other than their particular localities. The name was, in turn, adopted by a Chinese nationalist warlord in Xinjiang in 1934 upon the suggestion of his Soviet adviser. The six million oasis-dwelling Turkic Muslims in Xinjiang gladly revived it, since this acceptance brought with it recognition by the state as an autonomous region. For the Uighur people, this reaffirmation of their ethnic identity struck a deep chord in their sense of unity. The Uighur are now one of the 55 official minority groups in China and are recognized throughout the Republics of the former Soviet Union.

"Uighur people all can sing, and most play some kind of folk instruments. Every family has at least one 'dutar' (lute). Uighurs cannot have a party without singing and dancing."

KAN BERI DOLKUN
PhD candidate at Columbia University, originally from Xinjiang

"Due to the political situation in China, the texts of many songs were rewritten to fit Party standards. But in our homes, we never stopped singing the songs as they used to be. Regardless of the political situation, the song texts were remembered. Even though restrictions are not as great as they once were, we are discriminated against in every respect. By American standards of human rights, we have none. By Chinese standards, we have some. Our situation is really not very different from that of Tibet. Still our music is something that cannot be taken away. It's different than any other music."

KAN BERI DOLKUN

Music remains an important part of life for the Uighur. Not only are their lives accompanied by the music of the *sazanda* ~ professional musicians hired to play at births, circumcisions, weddings and religious festivals ~ but, unlike in many Islamic nations, amateur musicians are actively encouraged. Instruments are found in almost every home and are often played by children from a very young age. Singers are hired to accompany farmers in the fields, wandering merchants chant religious hymns in the bazaars, and virtually any social gathering can be transformed into a *mashrap*, a celebration in which music and dance are the focus.

Uighur folk songs are popular throughout the Tarim Basin. The subject of these songs is almost invariably love. The more formal musical tradition of the Uighur people is expressed in the classical *muqam*, which serves for Uighurs as a symbol of their cultural inheritance.

Long-necked lutes, favored by the Turkic peoples, predominate in the music of the Uighurs. Several fiddles are played in the Tarim basin as well. The piercing sound of the *sunai*, a double-reed instrument made of brass or wood, is a conspicuous feature of most outdoor festivals. It is often played in a duo with kettle drums, called *naghra*.

DISC 2
TRACK 4
The folk song, "*Nazirkhom*" is performed by a traditional Uighur duo of *sunai* and *naghra*. These duos have have their roots in processions and military campaigns. This recording was made in Xinjiang, China, in 1987.

KAYAPO

In villages scattered along the Xingu River in central Brazil, the Kayapo Indians have long taken pride in their fighting ability. While initially this prowess was demonstrated in raids on other tribes or skirmishes within their ranks, Kayapo warrior skills have proven useful for well over a hundred years against a steady stream of gold miners, rubber workers, Brazil-nut gatherers, hunters and land speculators. These forces have encroached on the rainforest, whose delicate ecosystem the Kayapo have expertly managed for hundreds of years.

Contests over the land and the natural resources of the middle Xingu river basin began well before roads and airstrips penetrated the area in the 1970s and '80s. The first major battles were fought over one hundred years ago between settlers and a remarkable group of Indians called the Kayapo, a warrior tribe whose people survived long after many other groups had perished. Beginning in the 1970s, the Kayapo waged a successful campaign to secure the borders of their territory, and in so doing they underwent a rapid process of cultural transformation. Once a barely organized collection of village groups with little tradition of tribal unity, they emerged as articulate and internationally known leaders of a powerful indigenous movement in Amazonia. Through sophisticated political negotiations and the skilled use of the media, the Kayapo were successful in securing ~ even expanding ~ the borders of their territory.

excerpt from Marianne Schmink and Charles H. Wood, "Contested Frontiers in Amazonia"

The Kayapo warrior tradition is now a powerful symbol used to make nonviolent statements. On several occasions, hundreds of Kayapo Indians~in warpaint, wielding clubs ~ put on spectacular demonstrations to call attention to issues of indigenous rights.

In addition to the notoriety the Kayapo have received for their political action, a great deal of attention is now being paid to their sophisticated use of their land. Their soil management practices have, in fact, been proven to be much more productive than those of colonists or ranchers in the region.

The Kayapo of Brazil practice seed selection, fertilization of the soil and crop rotation.... Garden clearings contain a wide range of trees and plants, of various sizes and with different rates of growth. Some are harvested after several months or even several years. Others will continue to provide for up to 40 years and are visited long after the village has abandoned its site.

excerpt from Julian Burger,
"The Gaia Atlas of First Peoples"

"THE KAYAPO USED TO DEFEND THEMSELVES WITH WAR CLUBS AND SPEARS. TODAY, WE DEFEND OURSELVES WITH WORDS, OUR HEADS AND THE PRESS."

KAYAPO CHIEF

Despite their many contacts with the modern world, the Kayapo maintain much of their ceremonial life. Body painting ~ which is both cosmetic and symbolic ~ is a part of traditional daily attire. Adults paint each other in groups, and women spend hours decorating their children. The traditional symbol of Kayapo manhood ~ a wooden mouth disc ~ however, is worn today by only a few of the older men.

Kayapo life involves a litany of ritual ceremonies. The Kayapo are usually in the midst of one ceremony or making preparations for the next.

For Kayapo, there are individual naming ceremonies; rituals associated with hunting, fishing, and agriculture; and rites of passage from one age class to the next. All of these ceremonies are designated by the generic term *"me rer mex,"* meaning "the people who show off beautifully." This refers not only to the elaborate ornaments worn by participants, but to the festive ceremonies themselves, held in village squares.

Corn is the staple food of the rainy season, and it is the crop which gives rise to the most important rituals. The corn festival, *bàyjangri*, is celebrated each year to ensure a good harvest. It starts when the seedlings appear, and continues over a period of three months. During the ceremony, adult men perform three all-night dances. Each dance is preceded by a small hunting expedition to provide meat as well as ceremonial ornaments.

Each dance has its own songs, which are performed exclusively by men, frequently in a high falsetto voice. Daily rehearsals are organized by village elders; they determine the proper arrangement of verses and orchestrate, with elaborate precision, the entire ceremony. These days, Kayapo men frequently accompany singers at their ceremonies with tape recorders in hand, capturing their songs for later study.

"No'ôk-'ãmõr," or *"Learning the songs of the Corn,"* was recorded during preparations for a *hàyjangri*, a corn ceremony in a forest camp of Kayapo *Mekrãgnotí* Indians. The Mekrãgnotí are a tribe of the Kayapo whose name means, "people with the large red facial painting." This particular song accompanies a dance in which participants wear elaborate body paint as well.

Tolai

The Tolai people live on the Gazelle Peninsula of New Britain, northeast of the mainland of Papua New Guinea. Though they were reported to be living a stone-age lifestyle well into the 19th century, the Tolai are today regarded as one of the most sophisticated and advanced people of the whole of the independent territory of Papua New Guinea.

The Gazelle Peninsula was named after a German exploration vessel, the Gazelle, which operated in the area in the late 1800s. Many European vessels sailed past the Peninsula during the 19th century, yet the Tolai acquired little from these passing ships other than a knowledge of the power of their guns. European traders and missionaries began to arrive in the 1870s. The peninsula was eventually annexed by the German Empire. Good climate, fertile soils and a magnificent bay harbor offered settlers ideal conditions for plantation colonies. The Tolai experienced great changes in their lives. After World War I, the area came under Australian rule by mandate of the League of Nations.

The pace and social development of the territory's population in general and of the Tolai in particular has accelerated since World War II. The Tolai were quick to create a modern governmental structure. The first native local government council in all of New Guinea was formed in the Tolai area in 1950. In 1960, the first elected officials joined the legislative council. Three years later, universal adult voting rights were enacted, and a democratically elected House of Assembly was introduced. The two separate territories of Papua, on the southern portion of the island, and New Guinea, on the northern, were gradually consolidated and their joint name became official in 1971. Australia granted Papua New Guinea its independence in 1979.

Tolai religion involves a vast array of spirits referred to by the collective term "*tabaran*." "Denizens of the bush" are grotesque, malevolent and much feared elements. "Spirits of the air" are benign figures, whose help is sought by those composing songs, designing costumes, or choreographing dances for a ceremony.

The *"tubuan"* is a being represented by a conical mask and a dress of leaves, each with its own design. Its spirit lies at the heart of the Tolai religious system.

The tubuan is "raised" to dance at a variety of festivals. The great climactic Tolai rite is the *matamatam*, a ceremony to honor all the deceased of the clan, in which masked figures of tubuan appear.

The tubuan is more than a mere ritual and dance performer. Traditional Tolai

"IN PAPUA NEW GUINEA, YOU FIND MANY ISOLATED VILLAGES WHICH MAINTAIN AGE-OLD TOTEM BELIEFS AND MYTHOLOGY. THEY'VE COME TO REALIZE THAT THEIR TRADITIONAL CULTURE IS WORTH PRESERVING."

WARREN FAHEY
producer and folklorist

THE TUBUAN DANCE IS EXTRAORDINARY BOTH MUSICALLY AND VISUALLY. ELABORATE BODY PAINTINGS AND SPECTACULAR COSTUMES ACHIEVE A STAGGERING EFFECT.

believed it was the king in its sphere of influence. Early writers described it as judge, policeman and hangman all in one. Each clan or lineage may have one or two of these tubuan. To outsiders, all tubuan look alike, but Tolai villagers can distinguish one from another. The Tolai have a Tubuan season. The Tubuan are said to be "revived" at the beginning, and will be "killed" at the end of the season.

In coastal villages, at the beginning of the season, a canoe dance is performed by the tubuan in the water. Usually, every evening during the season, the men sit on the edge of the dancing ground with their kudu drums and garamut slit-drums. A short tune is played with the garamut calling the tubuan to appear.

Once in the dancing ground, the men begin to play their kudu and to sing. The Tubuan dances to the music. This continues for a whole evening, into the early morning. Each song is different than the previous although very much the same in musical style. These songs are specifically for Tubuan dances, and they cannot be used for other ceremonies. It is also forbidden to sing them at all without the accompaniment of a dancing Tubuan.

JACOB SIMET
excerpt from liner notes to "Papua New Guinea: Tolai Traditional Music from the Gazelle Peninsula"

DISC 2
TRACK 6
"Akuka," a men's dance, is part of the ceremony to *"raise the tubuan."* It was recorded in Vunavail, Papua New Guinea. The group performing on this track consists of eleven men accompanied by four *kudu* drums.

AGA

cano which is the stepping stone to Balinese Hinduism's presiding deity, Ida Sanghyang Widhi Wasa.

*excerpt from David Lewiston,
liner notes to "Bali: Gamelan & Kecak"*

Few places on earth are as abundantly blessed as the island of Bali, situated at the southeastern tip of Java in the Indonesian archipelago. The fertile hillsides of this small island are sculpted into verdant rice paddies, dotted with villages whose houses and temples are in harmonious proportion to the countryside, the whole dominated by the lofty peak of Gunung Agung, the vol-

The Aga are one of several cultures indigenous to the island of Bali. Their most important village is named Tenganan, meaning "halfway from the sea to the hills." Its people maintain the island's most ancient traditions, which predate the influx of Javanese aristocrats in the 15th century. Tenganan is primarily a ceremonial village, concerned mainly with the observance of religious ritual. The community, relatively wealthy by Balinese standards, employs outsiders to farm its large land holdings.

The Aga people are a tiny minority of all Balinese. Aga villages are secluded and have little contact with neighboring peoples. In Tenganan, strict caste rules require anyone who marries an outsider to leave the village. Many young people, who find life in

Tenganan too constricting, have been moving away from the village. Tenganan's population, which numbered less than 300 in 1988, continues to decline.

In Bali, the word *gamelan* can refer to a small ensemble of four or five musicians, or to an orchestra of forty. Gamelan consist of only the most respected musicians. Their metallophones, gongs, flutes and drums are all carefully tuned for specific occasions.

The *gamelan salunding* is the most ancient musical ensemble arrangement in Bali; some believe it to be two thousand years old. The music it produces, hauntingly beautiful and complex, is performed on metallophones made of iron, instead of the more typical bronze. Gamelan salunding is considered especially sacred. It accompanies a women's dance performed as an offering to the gods. The Aga have a legend, in fact, whereby the first three notes of the gamelan salunding were provided by the gods.

"After two decades, I could no longer resist Bali's pull. Things had certainly changed. I landed at a bustling modern airport, a far cry from the ramshackle old landing field with a couple of propeller planes…. But the island had a delightful surprise in store for me; for the first time, I heard the hauntingly beautiful music of the gamelan salunding, Bali's most ancient ensemble. As I listened, the bell-like sounds of this gamelan wove a spell about me, the old spell of wonder which had drawn me to Bali so long ago."
DAVID LEWISTON

DISC 2
TRACK 5
"Gending Sekar Gadung," a song about the Gadung flower is performed by a *gamelan salunding*, directed by I Nyoman P. Gunawan. The recording was made by David Lewiston in Tenganan, Bali in 1987.

TURKMEN

and parts of China. The term Turkmen enters the historical records over 1,000 years ago. In Iran, where they are one of twelve major ethnic groups, Turkmen are concentrated in the northeastern steppe, near the Caspian Sea.

The Turkmen people live primarily in Turkmenistan — now one of the independent republics of the former Soviet Union~ as well as in Iran, Afghanistan

Despite the restrictive policies of the governments in Iran, the former Soviet Union and China, Turkmen traditions, especially their musical ones, remain vital.

"In Iran at the time of the Shah, Turkmen music was considered primitive. People were more interested in Western influences and more sophisticated sounds than an old man playing dutar."

"Attempts by the government to control or restrict Turkmen culture in Iran and other parts of the world cannot really be effective. You have to realize that the state is a monolith, and that ethnic groups are made up of individuals. It is difficult for the state to get into the fabric of a culture. Individuals will always improvise, whether the state likes it or not."

MEHRDAD IZADY
Professor, Harvard University

Turkmen music places a strong emphasis on instrumental improvisation. Ornamentation is part of the text of songs, and the expression of human feelings is considered more important than meticulous adherence to rules.

The main musical instruments in Turkmen music are the *dutar*, a lute most commonly with two strings, the *tuiduk*, a flute, and the *dili-tuiduk*, a single-reed pipe. Dutar music is especially beloved by the Turkmen, and the instrument characterizes their folk songs. A typical folk song features a long introduction on dutar, followed by an intense, high-pitched vocal.

"The songs focus on love or loss, but a listener should be keenly aware that they use symbols. There is almost always a double meaning at work. If you take the text at face value, often you will miss the real meaning. A song that appears to be about worldly love, for instance, could very easily refer to religion. Historically, the music has tremendous religious significance and powerful therapeutic effect."

G. JANATI-ATAIE
Doctor of Music, New York University

"Since the revolution in Iran, folk music has become more popular. The tables have been turned. Now, city-based music for pleasure is considered sinful, and folk music has become art. Also, many younger people with Western educations are beginning to realize the value of their ethnic heritages."

MEHRDAD IZADY

DISC 2
TRACK 8

This traditional Turkmen song was recorded at Vahdat Symphony Hall in Teheran, Iran. The performers and song title are not known.

BATAK

Toba, Karo, Dairi-Pakpak, Simalungun, Angkola and *Mandailing*. Though divided by their religion and language, these ethnic groups are unified by a common passion for genealogy. It is not uncommon, for instance, to meet a Batak man who can recite the names of two centuries of ancestry. In fact, ancestry forms a blueprint for all of Batak society, and provides the basis for clans that dominate Batak life. Even today, Batak people identify much more with ancestral clans than with the ethnic groupings favored by Westerners.

Seventy-five thousand years ago, a volcano erupted deep in the northern interior of Sumatra, an Indonesian island just south of Thailand, leaving behind a crater now known as Lake Toba. One hundred kilometers long, Lake Toba is the largest volcanic crater in the world. The fertile volcanic soils of its shores have supported intensive agriculture for millennia, and its great beauty has established it as one of Indonesia's largest tourist attractions. This is the original homeland of the Batak, a family of Indonesian ethnic groups that account for a majority of Sumatra's ten million citizens.

Western social scientists separate the Batak people into six major ethnic groups:

Marriage ties between clans are organized in a very specific manner. Groups are referred to as "wife-takers" and "wife-givers." Between any two clans the "givers" are deemed the spiritual and ritual superiors of their indebted, subordinate "takers." A group that has received women as brides from one group, in turn passes on sisters and daughters to a third group, alternating between the roles of "giver" and "taker."

BATAK ....

For Batak a "complete" life is realized when all of one's children have, themselves, had children. A special ceremony, *saur matua*, honoring the passing of someone who has lived such a life, moves from grief to thanksgiving to celebration.

Indonesia is an Islamic country, and while some Batak are Islamic, most are officially Christian owing to Dutch influence. Even so, it is the clan systems and ancestral spirits that form the basis of the Batak ritual celebrations which are still a focus of Batak life. Most Batak separate *adat*, custom, from *agama*, true religion. In this way they can remain pious monotheists and maintain their elaborate adat ceremonies as well.

Most Batak ceremonies are associated with key events in the cycle of life, such as birth, marriage, and death. Ceremonies for the deceased are especially important. Most significant is the ritual disinternment and reburial of ancestral bones, seen as the last obligation of the living to their forebearers.

Batak ceremonies always involve music-making. In fact, the Batak word for ceremony, *gondang*, refers to the Batak orchestra as well as to the individual songs they play. The most prestigious Toba ensemble is the Gondang Sabangunan, consisting of *taganing*, a set of five tuned drums, *sarune bolon*, a type of double-reed instrument, and *ogung*, a set of four gongs. Other gondang may include mandolin, xylophone and flute.

"Musicians are essential to a ceremony because they are the intermediaries between humanity and the Creator. The sound of the drums and gongs convey human prayers to the spirit world. Musicians thus command great respect in traditional Batak society and must follow a certain code of behavior. 'The musicians must be honest men,' explained one old Toba Batak man, 'otherwise they risk angering the spirits.'"

MARC PERLMAN

"I went to one ceremony where people became possessed by spirits. Afterward, I was to interview the ceremonial practitioner, who insisted we join him for lunch. He had just come out of a deep trance, and here he was, a short while later, leading Christian Grace before the meal."

MARC PERLMAN
Visiting Professor, Tufts University

AT MOST CEREMONIES, PARTICIPANTS PERFORM "TORTOR," A DANCE USUALLY DONE WITH FEET IN PLACE AND HANDS TOGETHER, FINGERTIPS TOUCHING.

DISC 2
TRACK 9
"*Batara Guru*" is performed by a *Gondang Sabangunan*. Recorded at a performance in California, this piece is played as it would be at a traditional Toba ceremony. The master of ceremonies formally requests each piece with a short speech, punctuated by drumrolls.

WODAABE

"hakkilo," care and forethought. This code, along with our many taboos, was given to us by our ancestors. In fact, Wodaabe means, "people of the taboo."

MAKAO
Wodaabe man, excerpt from Marion van Offelen and Carol Beckwith, "Nomads of Niger"

The Wodaabe are members of the Fulani ethnic groups, whose once-nomadic population of six million are now mostly settled; only the Wodaabe, who today number about 50,000, remain nomadic. They are widely scattered across the sub-Sahara Sahelian steppe in the West African republic of Niger.

As their nomadic desert life dictates, the Wodaabe are accustomed to getting by with very little and to sharing whatever they have. What they value more than anything else are personal relationships.

Tradition is friendship, it is mutual assistance, it is respect for others. In our tradition, we have a code of behavior which emphasizes "semteende", reserve and modesty; "munyal," patience and fortitude; and

Numerous and rigid taboos are steadfastly observed by the Wodaabe. When Wodaabe greet one another, they are forbidden to make eye contact. A man may not hold his wife's hand in public, nor call her by name, nor speak to her in a personal way. A mother is forbidden from speaking to or calling by name her first-born child.

"What you love, you respect, and therefore you do not show that you love it."

MAKAO

Wodaabe men must marry within their own lineage, and this marriage, arranged at childhood is called a *kobgal* marriage. These marriages form the foundation of Wodaabe social institutions and add new

A GROUP OF WODAABE MEN ASSEMBLE IN A LINE IN FRONT OF THREE YOUNG WOMEN WHO ARE KNEELING. THE MEN'S FACES ARE PAINTED WITH YELLOW POWDER. BLACK LINES OUTLINE THEIR EYES AND MOUTH, EMPHASIZING THE WHITENESS OF THEIR TEETH AND EYES. WHITE LINES RUNNING FROM FOREHEAD TO CHIN ELONGATE THEIR NOSES. OSTRICH FEATHERS AND HORSETAIL PLUMES HIGHLIGHT THEIR ELABORATE COS-TUMES. AS THE MEN CHANT AND CLAP, THEY STRUT AND PREEN, SHOUL-DER TO SHOULDER, AS IN A CHORUS LINE. THEY ROLL THEIR EYES AND CLICK THEIR TEETH. HUNDREDS OF FELLOW WODAABE, ONLOOKERS, SUR-ROUND THEM. THE GEEREWOL DANCES HAVE BEGUN.

members to the lineage. But Wodaabe men are also free to choose partners from other lineages, and they often elope to pursue these *teegal* marriages.

The Wodaabe say that their original ancestors, Adam and Adama, handed them great natural beauty as their inheritance. They believe that they are the most beautiful people on earth.

In addition to their physical beauty their attractions to one another are based on *togu*, or charm. A man's togu is enhanced by *magani*, a potion or medicine, which the Wodaabe drink, eat, wear and rub on their clothes.

The highlight of Wodaabe social life comes once a year during the *Duungu* period when the rains finally fall. The Wodaabe's constant struggle for survival in the desert temporarily lifts. They have time to celebrate, to sing and to dance. This is when the Geerewol celebrations are held.

Two lineages of Wodaabe unite for seven days filled with dancing. The focus is on male beauty and sexual attraction. Dominating the festivities are the *Geerewol* dances, at which handsome young men vie for the honor of being chosen the most charming and most beautiful, to prove their outstanding ability to attract women.

In preparation for the Geerewol dances, Wodaabe men spend hours creating elaborate makeup and costumes. They then line up to perform for three unmarried women, chosen as judges by the elders, and a group of onlookers.

The men begin to intone a chant, which continues as they dance to the accompaniment of unison singing. Clapping hands and jingling metal anklets provide the rhythm. The chants of the Geerewol dancers are believed to awaken the potions they have taken, which "rise to the heart and show themselves in the blood."

The winners reap the intangible rewards of increased pride, the admiration of other men, and the ardor of women. Romantic unions and teegal marriages spring from the ceremony, too, signaled with eye contact and consummated in the bush.

"The first thing the men did was to gather up chameleons from the desert, dry them and grind them for makeup. They believe this will transform them, just as the rains have transformed their homeland. I couldn't believe how much the Wodaabe and the entire desert were transformed. It was intensely moving."

CAROL BECKWITH
photographer and author

DISC 2
TRACK 10
"Lelore" was recorded in Dakoro, Niger, at the *Geerewol* celebrations during the rainy season of 1983.

NATIVE AMERICANS

tions that revolve around a profound reverence for native lands and animals.

"I operate with two different sets of values and behaviors. One for American culture and one for my home."

ARLIE NESKAHI
a Navajo singer living in Los Angeles

The Navajo herds his sheep in the vast silence of a Southwestern plateau. High on a mesa, the Hopi enacts his traditional pleas for rain. The Seminole paddles his canoe through the waters of the Everglades. Mohawk steelworkers make their way along girders of skyscrapers above New York City traffic. Zuni and Apache are flown to fight forest fires in western states. A Pueblo musician explains his art in an Arizona public school.

Throughout the United States and Canada, Native Americans, or American Indians ~ the indigenous people of North America ~ pursue lives that are an intricate weave of present-day technology and media with thousand-year-old tradi-

Since white settlers first arrived in North America, Native Americans have seen their land taken away and their culture and beliefs threatened, even outlawed.

Today, Native Americans have a complex relationship with the government. Over 500 Indian "nations" are recognized by the United States. As individuals, every Native American has the constitutional rights enjoyed by all citizens. As nations, each has a formal relationship with the government based on treaties dating back, in some cases, hundreds of years. The U.S. Census Bureau estimates a population of

nearly two million Native Americans; of these, according to the Bureau of Indian Affairs, about half live on reservations. Only in the last two decades has this indigenous minority begun to gain back land rights and other guarantees contained in their treaties.

"We are carriers of an accumulated knowledge. When I sing, I feel a direct connection to hundreds of years and to all the singers who came before me.

ARLIE NESKAHI

The spiritual heritage of Native American people is here ~ it has not been extinguished. I believe the spiritual fire still burns and is beckoning for America, indeed to the world, to come closer, to listen, to learn, and to share in its warmth and comfort. It is time, that the buckskin curtain be drawn back. It is time, I know it…. Teach the children. The Grandfathers and the Grandmothers are in the children. If we educate them, our children tomorrow will be wiser than we are today. They're the Grandfathers and Grandmothers of tomorrow.

excerpt from Eddie Benton-Banai, Ojibway Nation, "Wisdomkeepers: Meetings with Native American Spiritual Elders"

The value of this music and dance to the peoples who created them and still use them cannot be overestimated. Indian music and dance pervade all aspects of life, from creation stories to death and remembrance of death. The importance of American Indian dance is found not only in its impact on modern society, but also in the traditions and values it expresses to and for the Indian peoples. This oral tradition has survived solely because the music and dance were too important to be allowed to die. Native peoples' relationships to their creators, their fellow humans, and to nature is what American Indian dance really celebrates.

excerpt from Charlotte Heth's introduction to "Native American Dance: Ceremonies and Social Traditions"

Native American music reflects traditions which intertwine spirituality and daily life. There are songs relating to every thing, every being and every activity, ranging from the commonplace and secular to the sacred and ceremonial.

Nearly all Native American music is vocal, sung alone or in choruses, usually

by men. These vocals are powerfully rhythmic, often featuring shouts and even animal calls.

"I'm tired of reading books and seeing movies that only depict Indians drumming. One of the things that distinguishes our music is that it is not beat-driven, not rhythm-driven, it is song-driven and melody-driven. We know the proper melodies of different spirits."

ARLIE NESKAHI

Though Native American music may be divided into many regional styles associated with specific nations, there exist some basic categories of songs across all regions.

Songs relating to everyday activities and children's games exist in all nations. They are purely secular, and may be sung by anyone at anytime.

"I wish I could travel back in time. There were songs for everything you did ~ when you woke up, when you washed, when you rode horses. There were songs everywhere and for every purpose."

ARLIE NESKAHI

"Powwow Songs" serve both social needs and spiritual desires. They represent a long tradition of community song and dance. "Spiritual Songs" are meant for singing in the "sweatlodge," a traditional sauna meant to purify body, mind and spirit.

"Ceremonial Songs" honor people, deities or nature. "Healing Songs" are usually sung only by ceremonial practitioners, who apprentice for years, learning precise performance styles and specific song sequences. "Sacred Songs" are directly connected to the spirits and may be sung only by certain singers in specific circumstances.

"We are not allowed to perform these religious songs in the wrong context. Songs such as the Corn Dance and Deer Dance are only for certain times of the year. They are 'power element' songs for Mother Earth, scientific songs for each season."

ROBERT MIRABAL
musician of the Taos Pueblo Nation

The term "powwow" originally referred to curing ceremonies. The term passed into English as a word referring to any Indian gathering or as a verb meaning "to confer in council." In Indian country, it came to mean "a secular event featuring group singing and social dancing by men, women and children." Although many of its elements are traditional, powwows have changed considerably over time, and today serve as dynamic expressions of Native American identity and pride.

"Powwows have become the mainstream American way of categorizing Native peoples. It's important to realize that there are many different tribes that traditionally had

nothing to do with powwows. The influence of media and new modes of travel has changed that. Today, powwows represent a new way of sharing.'

ROBERT MIRABAL

Years ago, powwows were regionalized, but now they serve as pan-tribal events, featuring a wide range of songs, dances, contests and games. On the surface, the powwow appears as a social event and, on one level, it is. But there is always a protocol of a spiritual nature observed. People come to reflect and to pray, as well as to dance and compete.

For Native Americans, the singer and the drum ~ a term used to refer to a group of singers and a drummer ~ are elemental to the connections between past, present and future, and to the ties that bind all living things.

DISC 2
TRACK 11

This *"Stick Game Song,"* performed by the Bad Canyon Wellpinit Singers of Spokane, Washington, is part of a traditional gambling game. There are many regional variations of the "stick game." In each, two teams play against one another, alternately hiding and locating an item. The teams compete in singing as well ~ usually the better the song and the stronger the voices, the better the odds of victory.

TRACK 12

"Navajo Squaw Dance," is sung by legendary Navajo singer Edward Lee Natay. Squaw Dances last four days, with festivities held at a different location each night. When *"Natay: Navajo Singer,"* the album containing this track, was first released by Canyon Records in 1951, it was promoted at the Arizona State Fair. *Newsweek* reported, "Nodding and smiling, the Indians began to buy record albums, some as many as a half dozen, to take back to the reservation."

TRACK 13

This *"Squaw Dance Song"* is performed by The Northern Cree Singers of Saskatchewan, Canada. It was recorded at the 23rd Annual Northern Ute Powwow, in Fort Duchesne, Utah by Robert Doyle.

WAGOGO

"I have fled from hilltop to hilltop right up to Chigwe, but hunger follows me everywhere all the time."

from a Wagogo song

The Wagogo live on a high plateau located in the heart of Tanzania. Until the 18th century, they existed in almost total isolation, avoiding the influence of Arab merchants and the administration of the Sultan of Oman in Zanzibar. It was the ivory trade that eventually opened their land to the outside world two centuries ago.

In the clan system of Wagogo society there is no central authority. The Wagogo live in small villages of ten to twenty people. These hamlets are built on a temporary basis using wood and straw. Families move often, due to frequent droughts and famine. As with many cultures in this region, hunger is a persistent problem.

In the arid climate, their agriculture is limited to millet, sweet potatoes, squash and other gourds. Women tend the gardens, while cattle husbandry is reserved for the men. In the long hours spent following the herd, the Wagogo have developed a rich oral tradition, in which music is of great importance.

"Sung dances" accompany feast days and harvests, circumcision rites, market day gatherings and funerals for clan chieftains. They reveal an elaborate vocal repertoire, with complex harmonies distinct from those of other African cultures. Wagogo "entertainment" music is distinguished by the use of the *mbira*, a "hand piano" or "thumb piano," and *zeze*, which are small fiddles made from

gourds and hide. Mbira is an instrument popular in many parts of Africa. The Wagogo create and play the largest, with up to 40 keys, and are considered virtuosos on the instrument.

Each song begins with a short instrumental introduction, played on mbira or zeze.

Instruments then enter one after another, slowly building to a rich polyphony. Although traditional lyrics are still popular, present-day Wagogo musicians have adapted many songs in their traditional style to deal with political themes as a means of empowerment, and a way to enlarge their audience.

party's official ideology, summed up in the Swahili word *"ujamaa,"* aims to build an egalitarian society based on its own strength. It is an ideal the Wagogo embrace.

"Sote tulifurahia kama siku ya arusi," or, "We rejoiced as on our wedding day," is a song that celebrates the formation of the Tanganyika African National Union (TANU), a nationalist and anticolonial party founded in 1954. This party led the country to independence in 1965, and fused with Zanzibar's Afro Shirazi Party (ASP) to form the Chama Cha Mapinduzi (CCM), the "party of revolution." The

DISC 2
TRACK 14
"Sote tulifurahia kama siku ya arusi"
(lyrics to right)
is sung in *Swahili*,
rather than *Kigogo*
in order to reach a
broader audience.
Swahili, spoken by
more than 15 million
Tanzanians, is the
national language
of Tanzania.

"GREAT IS OUR JOY SINCE THE DAY WHEN TANU WAS FORMED
FOR TANU UNITED US AND LED US TO FREEDOM.
TRULY, TANU BROUGHT US THE LIGHT OF LOVE AND OF PEACE
WE FEEL AS FREE AS ON A WEDDING DAY.
O, THANK YOU TANU FOR UNITING US, WE ARE ALL REJOICING
O, THANK YOU AFRO FOR BRINGING US TOGETHER,
YOUR EXISTENCE AND YOUR DIRECTIONS-TANU-HAVE REINFORCED US
YOUR PRESENCE AND YOUR COMMAND-AFRO-HAVE STRENGTHENED US
WE HAVE GAINED BACK OUR SELF-ESTEEM
BY REJECTING ALL THOSE WHO SOLD US AND HUMILIATED US.
TODAY, THE ROLE OF THE PARTY IS TO OBSERVE THE CODE OF LEADERSHIP
AND ENCOURAGE RESPECT FOR IT,
TO ALLOW FOR THE ECONOMIC DEVELOPMENT OF THE COUNTRY
TO GUARANTEE THE SUCCESS OF OUR POLICY OF UJAMAA
TO SAVE THE DEMOCRACY OF THE PARTY
WHAT WAS THIS PREGNANCY?
O, IT WAS THAT OF TANU AND AFRO SHIRAZI.
YES, TRULY FROM THIS PREGNANCY THE CCM WAS BORN
ALL THE CHILDREN OF THE NATION COME FROM TANU AND AFRO SHIRAZI
O, GOD BE PRAISED, CCM EXISTS!
ALL THE THOUGHTS IN TANZANIA GO TOWARDS TANU AND AFRO SHIRAZI
O, GOD BE PRAISED, CCM EXISTS!"

AFTERWORD

The voices of indigenous people—direct descendants of the original inhabitants of their respective homes - are beginning to be heard above the din of societies which, all too often, have turned a deaf ear. Politically, they demand rights and representation. Environmentally, they defend that which they hold most dear—the land they've inherited. Culturally, they teach us ways to farm, to heal and to look at life. The voices heard through this project are powerful, too; they say simply, *"Our land sounds like this."*

No less present in this package are the voices of those like photographer Carol Beckwith, who spent three years in the desert with Wodaabe people; author Louis Sarno, who set off to capture beautiful Pygmy sounds and wound up falling in love; musician Jeffrey Worbeck, whose chance encounter with an aging Azerbaijani musician turned into a lifelong muse; and David Lewiston, whose globetrotting activities lend elegance to the self-appointed title of "musical tourist." These dedicated professionals and devoted non-professionals have themselves become part of the music and of the cultures they document and, in so doing, provide the seeds of future growth.

Certainly, these chapters are not intended as a compendium; they advance neither musicology nor ideology. Instead, they seek to add context and resonance to their accompanying music. They are glimpses and snapshots, mere hints of the whole.

Voices of Forgotten Worlds focuses on a method of communication well-suited to a global perspective. Music is a unique vehicle by which we can explore the foreign and the distant, free from the weight of political or moral baggage. This is due to a few simple facts: a good beat moves us, a song can make us laugh or cry, and it's damn fun to hear something entirely new.

There are countless ways in which we can relate to these peoples, and a variety of approaches we can take to the injustices and crises visited upon so many of them. It seems that the first and most significant action, though, is simply to listen.

LARRY BLUMENFELD

Ellipsis Arts…

ACKNOWLEDGMENTS

VOICES OF FORGOTTEN WORLDS WOULD NOT HAVE BEEN POSSIBLE WITHOUT THE GENEROUS ASSISTANCE OF THE FOLLOWING PEOPLE, INSTITUTIONS AND SERVICE ORGANIZATIONS.

SPECIAL HEARTFELT THANKS TO ALL OF THOSE WHOSE NAMES ARE TOO NUMEROUS TO MENTION, BUT WITHOUT WHOM THIS PROJECT COULD HAVE NEVER BEEN COMPLETED.

Jagdish Agarwal, Bryan & Cherry Alexander, Prof. Dr. Max Peter Baumann, Carol Beckwith, Maria Bodmann, Sheila Boncy, Dorothy Carrington, Gabriella Vargas-Centina, Ellen Charno, Jennifer Charno, Barbara Chernow, Rachel Cooper, Hjalmar Dahl, Clifford DeArment, Shahyara Deneshgar, Zoraida Diaz de, Monroy, Robert Doyle, Victor Englebert, Warren Fahey, Guy Garcia, Sylvia Blanco-Green, Aphrodite Jones, Andy Kay, Andy & Debbie Krikun, Dr. Wolfgang Laade, Betsey Lerner, Ted Levin, Eduardo Llerenas, Kasz Maciag, O.P. Malik, Karen Michel, Masoud Modarres, Arlie Neskahi, Terence O'Neill-Joyce, Phillip Page, Marc Perlman, Lars "Miki" Petersen, Bess Pruitt, Susan Reich, J.R. Rich, Adrian Ross, Thomas & Lorraine Sakata, Gary Todoroff, Marion van Offelen, Jeffrey Werbock, Charlie Winton.

Jeffrey Alford and Naomi Duguid, *Asia Access*
Professor Edward Allworth, *Middle East Asian Language & Culture Dept., Columbia University*
Elias Amare, *Eritrean Cultural Civic Center, Washington, DC*
American Indian Community
Myrdene Anderson, *Dept. of Sociology & Anthropology, Purdue University*
Robert Archibald, *Australian Overseas Information Service*
G. Janati-Ataie, *New York University*
Laurent Aubert, *Directeur, Ateliers d'ethnomusicologie*
Australian Consulate
Pierre Bois, *Inedit Records/ Maison des Cultures du Monde*
Victoria Bricker, *Tulane University*
Gaye Brown, *National Museum of the American Indian*
Robert Browning, *World Music Institute*
Canyon Records
Center for Iranian Studies, *Columbia University*
Larry Clark, *University of Indiana*
Lillian Davidson, *National Geographic Society*
Shahyar Deneshgar, *University of Indiana*
Kam Beri Dolkun, *Columbia University*
Philip Dominici, *North Shore Graphics Arts*
Embassy of Eritrea
Mary Farquharson, *Asociación para la Investigación de la Música Tradicional A.C.*
Jim Farrington, *Wesleyan University Music Library*

Dr. Steven Feld, *Dept. of Anthropology, University of Texas*
Nanci Gonzalez, *University of Maryland*
Steven Gorelick, *The Ladakh Project*
Michael Hauser, *The Royal Danish Academy of Music*
Charlotte Heth, *Associate Dean, School of Music, UCLA*
Te Rangi Huata, *Kahurangi Maori Dance Theatre*
Mehrdad Izady, *Harvard University*
Alfred Jakobsen, *Inuit Circumpolar Conference*
Kanak Cultural Center
Kwang Hwa Mass Communications
Pierre Laulanne, *Agence de Developpement de la Culture Kanak*
Robert Leavitt, *Cultural Survival*
Ralph Leighton, *Friends of Tuva*
David Levinson, *Human Relations Area Files*
The Libraries of Columbia University
Lindenmeyr Monroe of Long Island
Eric Marinitsch, *IMZ International Music Center*
David McAllester, *Professor Emeritus, Wesleyan University*
Ann P. McCauley, *Johns Hopkins University*
Carine Mitchell, *Encyclopedia of World Cultures*
New Zealand Embassy
Don Niles, *Cultural Research Center, Papua New Guinea*
Pan Records
Publishers Group West
Susan Rodgers, *Dept. of Anthropology, Holy Cross College*
Lorraine Sakata, *School of Music, University of Washington, Seattle*
Parker Shipton, *Harvard University*
S. Shpoon, *Voice of America*
Karsten Sommer, *ULO Records*
Sovfoto
Staff and Volunteers of the
United Nations Centre for Human Rights
Paul Titus, *University of California at Riverside*
United Nations Photo Library
Nicole Waia, *Radio Djiido, New Caledonia*
Norman Whitten, *University of Illinois*
Donna Winslow, *University of Montreal*
World Council of Indigenous Peoples

CREDITS

PHOTOGRAPHY

FRONT COVER
All photos courtesy of the United Nations except: upper left hand corner photo courtesy of David Lewiston and right hand column, fourth photo down, courtesy of Niillas A. Somby.

TUVANS
Pg. 16   Courtesy of Paradox

AINU
Pg. 19   Ian Berry/Magnum Photos Inc.
Pg. 20   Ian Berry/Magnum Photos Inc.

GARIFUNA
Pg. 23   Zoraida Diaz de Monroy
Pg. 25   Zoraida Diaz de Monroy

QUECHUAN
Pg. 27   Stephen Ferry/Gamma Liaison
Pg. 29   Victor Englebert

SAAMI
Pg. 31   B & C Alexander
Pg. 33   Niillas A. Somby

BUNUN
Pg. 35   Kwang Hwa Mass Communications
Pg. 37   Kwang Hwa Mass Communications

KANAK
Pg. 39   Copyright A.D.C.K./David Becker
Pg. 41   Copyright A.D.C.K./David Becker

AUSTRALIAN ABORIGINES
Pg. 43   Australian Overseas Information Service
Pg. 45   Harvey Lloyd/The Stock Market

PASHTUN
Pg. 47   S. Thomas Sakata
Pg. 48   S. Thomas Sakata

NEWAR
Pg. 50   Roland Neveu/Gamma Liaison
Pg. 52   Bill Wassman/The Stock Market

INUIT
Pg. 54   Tom Stewart /The Stock Market
Pg. 57   B & C Alexander

MAYA
Pg. 59   Robert Van Der Hilst/ Gamma Liaison
Pg. 61   Paul S. Howell/Gamma Liaison

AZERBAIJANI
Pg. 62   Jeffrey Werbock
Pg. 65   Tass from Sovfoto

MAORI
Pg. 67   New Zealand Embassy

RASHAIDA
Pg. 70   1981 Robert Caputo/Aurora
Pg. 71   Angela Fisher & Carol Beckwith/Robert Estall Photographs
Pg. 72   Angela Fisher & Carol Beckwith/Robert Estall Photographs

TIBETANS
Pg. 75   Pablo Bartholomew/Gamma Liaison

LADAKHIS
Pg. 79   Linde Waidhofer/Gamma Liaison

SOLOMON ISLANDERS
Pg. 83   Michael McCoy/Photo Researches

BA-BENJELLÉ PYGMIES
Pg. 85   Michael Nichols/Magnum Photos Inc.
Pg. 87   Scott Peterson/Gamma Liaison

UIGHUR
Pg. 89   Neal Gillette/The Stock Market

KAYAPO
Pg. 93   Rio Branco/Magnum Photos Inc.
Pg. 95   Rio Branco/Magnum Photos Inc.

LOLAI
Pg. 97   United Nations Photo Library
Pg. 98   Valos/Gamma Liaison

AGA
Pg. 100   Jacques Alexandre/Gamma Liaison
Pg. 101   Jeffrey Alford/Asia Access

TURKMEN
Pg. 103   Sina Productions Inc.
Pg. 105   Sina Productions Inc.

BATAK
Pg. 107   Rita Ariyoshi
Pg. 109   Rita Ariyoshi

WODAABE
Pg. 111   Victor Englebert
Pg. 113   Peter Carmichael, Aspect Picture Library/The Stock Market

NATIVE AMERICANS
Pg. 115   John Running
Pg. 117   John Running

WAGOGO
Pg. 121   Wendy Stone/Gamma Liaison
Pg. 122   Jean-Paul Dumontier/Maison des Cultures du Monde

TEXT

Quotes and excerpts are drawn from original interviews or as credited below.

GARIFUNA
Pg. 22   From SOJOURNERS OF THE CARIBBEAN, by Nanci L. Gonzalez, Published in 1988 by the University of Illinois Press.

QUECHUAN
Pg. 29   From the album *Music in the Andean Highlands/ Bolivia*, 1978 Museum Collection Berlin by Max Peter Baumann

AUSTRALIAN ABORIGINES
Pg. 42   From THE SONGLINES by Bruce Chatwin. Copyright ©1987 by Bruce Chatwin. Used by permission of Viking Penguin, a division of Penguin Books USA Inc. Estate of Bruce Chatwin. Used by permission of Jonathan Cape, UK.

INUIT
Pg. 56   From INUUSUTTUT NIPAAT 1 by Lars "Miki" Petersen. Copyright Atuakkiorfik ©1991

MAYA
Pg. 58   From "Forgotten But Not Gone" by Guy Garcia. *Time* Magazine, Aug. 9, 1993 Copyright ©1993 Time Inc, Reprinted by permission.
Pg. 58-59 Reprinted from INCIDENTS OF TRAVEL IN CENTRAL AMERICA, CHIAPAS AND YUCATAN, John Lloyd Stephens, Ed. by Karl Ackerman. Washington D.C.: Smithsonian Institution Press. By permission of the publisher. Copyright ©1993

Smithsonian Institution
Pg. 60   From Kevin Gossner's SOLDIERS OF THE VIRGIN: THE MORAL ECONOMY OF A COLONIAL MAYA REBELLION ©1992 University of Arizona Press
Pg. 61   From I, RIGOBERTA MENCHU... AN INDIAN WOMAN IN GUATEMALA, Edited by Elisabeth Burgos-Debray ©1984 Verso Publishing. Reprinted by permission.

LADAKHI
Pgs. 78, 80 Excerpted from INCONTEXT: *A Quarterly of Humane Sustainable Culture.* Subscriptions $24/year; single issues: $6; P.O. Box 11470, Bainbridge Island, WA 98110

SOLOMON ISLANDERS
Pg. 82   From PLES BLONG IUMI: SOLOMON ISLANDS, THE PAST FOUR THOUSAND YEARS Copyright ©1989, University of the South Pacific, Suva and Honiara. Edited by Hugh Laracy, Sam Alasia... (et al.)

BA-BENJELLÉ PYGMIES
Pgs. 84, 86 From SONGS FROM THE FOREST: MY LIFE AMONG THE BA-BENJELLÉ PYGMIES by Louis Sarno. ©1993 Houghton-Mifflin Company

KAYAPO
Pg. 92   From CONTESTED FRONTIERS IN AMAZONIA by Marianne Schmink and Charles H. Wood ©1992 Columbia University Press, New York. Reprinted with the permission of the publisher.
Pg. 93   Julian Burger, THE GAIA ATLAS

OF FIRST PEOPLES: A FUTURE FOR THE INDIGENOUS WORLD Copyright ©1990 Gaia Books Ltd., London

TOLAI
Pg. 97, 99   From the album *Tolai Traditional Music: Music from the Gazelle Peninsula.* ℗1977 Larrikin Records By Frederic Duvelle, Jacob Simet, and Apisai Enos

AGA
Pg. 100 From the Album *Bali: Gamelan & Kecak* by David Lewiston, ©1989 Elektra/Asylum/Nonesuch Records

WODAABE
Pg. 110   ©1983 Marion van Offelen NOMADS OF NIGER, Harry N. Abrams Inc., N.Y. All rights reserved.

NATIVE AMERICANS
Pg. 116   Copyright ©1990 Steve Wall and Harvey Arden from the book WISDOMKEEPERS, Beyond Words Publishing, Hillsboro, Oregon, USA
Pg. 116   Heth, Charlotte, ed. NATIVE AMERICAN DANCE: CEREMONIES AND SOCIAL TRADITIONS. Washington, D.C.: Smithsonian Institution and Starwood Publishing, 1992.

WAGOGO
Pg. 123   Lyrics from the album *Tanzania: Songs of the Wagogo and Kuria.* Inedit/Maison des Cultures du Monde (Paris) CD W260041 ©1992 MCM

DATE DUE

SEP 30 00	
DEC 20 00	
FEB 1 2 2001	
MAR 0 4 2006	
FEB 1 1 2010	